zulu war 1879

twilight of a warrior nation

IAN KNIGHT & IAN CASTLE

zulu war 1879

twilight of a warrior nation

Praeger Illustrated Military History Series

Westport, Connecticut
London

PRAEGER

Library of Congress Cataloging-in-Publication Data

Knight, Ian, 1956–
    Zulu War 1879 / Ian Knight.
        p. cm. – (Praeger illustrated military history, ISSN 1547-206X)
    Originally published: Oxford: Osprey, 1992.
    Includes bibliographical references and index.
    ISBN 0-275-98628-4 (alk. paper)
    1. Zulu War, 1879. I. Title. II. Series
    DT1875.K5866   2005
    968.4'045 – dc22   2004062420

British Library Cataloguing in Publication Data is available.

First published in paperback in 1992 by Osprey Publishing Limited,
Midland House, West Way, Botley, Oxford OX2 0PH, UK
443 Park Avenue South, New York, NY 10016, USA

Library of Congress Catalog Card Number: 2004062420
ISBN: 0-275-98628-4
ISSN: 1547-206X

Praeger Publishers, 88 Post Road West, Westport, CT 06881
An imprint of Greenwood Publishing Group, Inc.
www.praeger.com

Printed in China through World Print Ltd.

The paper used in this book complies with the Permanent Paper Standard issued
by the National Information Standards Organization (Z39.48-1984).

10 9 8 7 6 5 4 3 2 1

FRONT COVER: **Author's collection**

CONTENTS

ORIGINS OF THE WAR

When the final shot had been fired at the battle of Ulundi on 4 July 1879, the Zulu army, which had been buoyed up by the great victory at Isandlwana at the start of the war, but then demoralized by the crushing defeat at Khambula, finally accepted that it was beaten, and that the war was over. That final shot was also the culmination of two years of hectic political activity aimed at clearing a major obstacle in the path of advancing British Imperialism in southern Africa.

Zululand had emerged as a strong and aggressive kingdom during the reign of King Shaka kaSenzangakhona, early in the nineteenth century. The first white settlers had arrived during Shaka's reign, however, and by the 1870s, Zululand had been hemmed in on two sides by the rapid expansion of European colonial communities; the British in Natal to the south, and the Boers of the republic of the Transvaal to the west. The coming of the whites had not always been peaceful, and the Zulu state had suffered from a number of ruinous wars which sapped its economic and military strength. In 1873, however, a new Zulu king, Cetshwayo kaMpande, initiated a programme of internal reforms aimed at revitalizing the state apparatus. The timing was unfortunate: at the same time his neighbours were coming to regard the existence of his kingdom as a threat to their own interests in the region. It was, therefore, only a matter of time before the different aspirations of the two nations, British and Zulu, brought them to contention, and ultimately confrontation.

The British, who had taken control of the Cape in 1806 for strategic reasons during the Napoleonic Wars, had found it an expensive possession. The constant squabbles between the British, Boers (the descendants of the original Dutch settlers), and various African groups had led to incessant petty warfare which had proved a drain on both the Treasury and the War Department. In the 1870s,

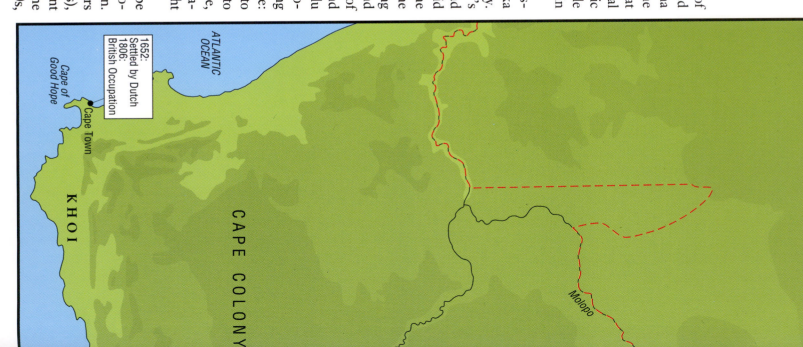

ATLANTIC OCEAN

Cape of Good Hope

Cape Town

1652: Settled by Dutch
1806: British Occupation

K H O I

C A P E   C O L O N Y

Molopo

Colonial Authority in South Africa, 1806-1880

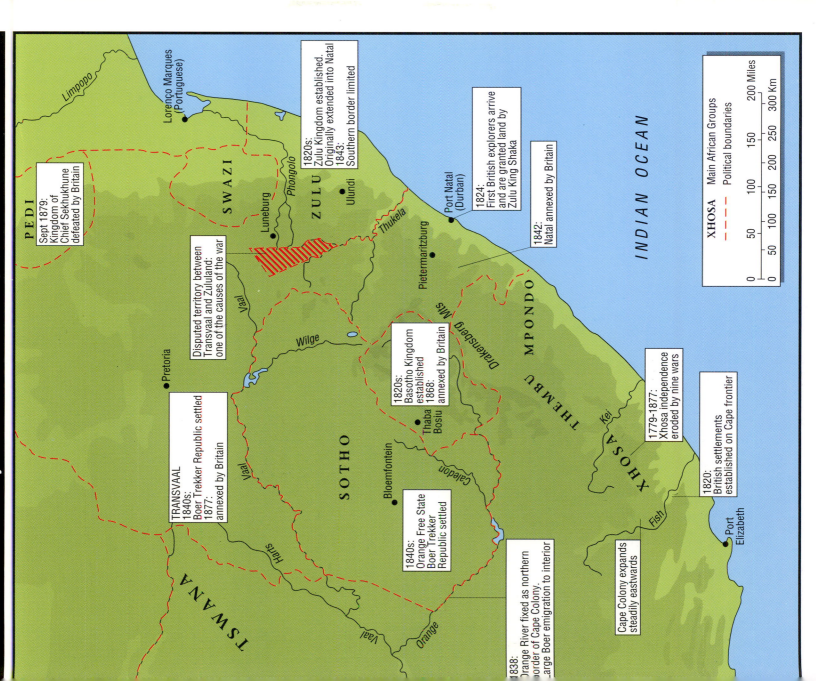

PEDI

Sept 1879:
Kingdom of
Chief Sekhukhune
defeated by Britain

Limpopo

Lorenço Marques
(Portuguese)

SWAZI

1820s:
Zulu Kingdom established.
Originally extended into Natal
1843:
Southern border limited

Luneburg

Phongolo

ZULU

Ulundi

Port Natal
(Durban)

1824:
First British explorers arrive
and are granted land by
Zulu King Shaka

1842:
Natal annexed by Britain

INDIAN OCEAN

Disputed territory between
Transvaal and Zululand:
one of the causes of the war

Vaal

Thukela

Pietermaritzburg

Wilge

Pretoria

MPONDO

Drakensberg Mts

1820s:
Basotho Kingdom
established
1868:
annexed by Britain

Thaba
Bosiu

THEMBU

1779-1877:
Xhosa independence
eroded by nine wars

Kei

TRANSVAAL
1840s:
Boer Trekker Republic settled
1877:
annexed by Britain

Vaal

SOTHO

Caledon

Bloemfontein

XHOSA

1820:
British settlements
established on Cape frontier

TSWANA

Harts

1840s:
Orange Free State
Boer Trekker
Republic settled

Fish

Cape Colony expands
steadily eastwards

Port
Elizabeth

1838:
Orange River fixed as northern
border of Cape Colony.
Large Boer emigration to interior

Vaal

Orange

XHOSA   Main African Groups
- - - - - Political boundaries

0   50   100   150   200 Miles
0   50   100 150 200 250 300 Km

they attempted to resolve these conflicts by adopting a policy known as Confederation, which proposed to unite the various rival black and white groups under a single – British – authority.

In 1877 Sir Henry Bartle Frere was installed as the new High Commissioner for South Africa, with the express intention of implementing Confederation. Frere very quickly became convinced that the Zulu kingdom posed the greatest single threat to the scheme. He became obsessed with the idea that Cetshwayo was behind a wave of unrest which was sweeping through the black population across South Africa, and began a propaganda campaign to pave the way for military intervention. Cetshwayo was described as an 'irresponsible, bloodthirsty and treacherous despot', and his warriors as 'celibate, man-slaying machines'. By this time, however, the home government was entangled in a crisis in the Balkans and a serious war in Afghanistan, and it was opposed to a new war in Africa. Frere was told to treat the Zulus with 'a spirit of forbearance'. His policy was too far advanced for him to abandon it, however, and he pressed on with his plans.

In March 1878 Lieutenant-General the Honourable Sir Frederic Thesiger – who was to become Lord Chelmsford on the death of his father in October of that year – took command of the Imperial forces in South Africa. Chelmsford agreed with Frere that a war with the Zulus was inevitable. Frere now had the means of prosecuting a war against the Zulus, and all he needed was an excuse. By manipulating the poor communications system between Cape Town and London, he hoped to present the home government with a *fait accompli*.

Frere found the justification he sought in reports of several minor border infringements. These incidents were of themselves innocuous – on one occasion a small party of Zulus had pursued some fugitives across the Mzinyathi river into Natal and dragged them back into Zululand; on another Colonial officials who had strayed into Zululand were temporarily detained as spies. Frere, however, siezed on these incidents as proof of the aggressive intentions of the Zulu king.

On 11 December 1878 King Cetshwayo's representatives were summoned to a meeting at the Lower Drift on the Thukela river, to receive the findings of a Boundary Commission, which had been arbitrating in a dispute concerning rival Boer and Zulu claims to a slice of territory along the Ncome (Blood) River. Britain had annexed the bankrupt Boer republic of the Transvaal in 1877 – much to the disgust of many of its inhabitants – and this dispute had been instrumental in shaping Frere's attitude towards the Zulu 'threat'. Contrary to his expectations, the Commission had found in favour of the Zulus, but the High Commissioner had taken the opportunity to make their findings conditional upon the Zulu acceptance of his demands. These included compensation for the border incidents, and, more seriously, the abandonment of the Zulu military system. If the Zulus did not comply within thirty days, it would be war. The demands were impossible, since they struck at the core of the Zulu way of life. Frere knew this; he counted on it. However willing King Cetshwayo might be to placate the British, Zulu society could not withstand the sudden disbandment of the military system. The die was cast.

▼ A water-colour by Orlando Norie of the 1st Battalion, 13th Light Infantry, on the march during the Zulu War. The 1/13th were part of Wood's Column. (Somerset L. I. Museum, Taunton)

OPPOSING STRATEGIES

The British Plan

Lord Chelmsford's strategy was shaped by his need to protect Natal and the Transvaal from a possible Zulu invasion, while at the same time confronting the Zulu army with sufficient force to destroy it. Since the home government had not sanctioned an offensive campaign, the forces at his disposal were limited. He distributed them at five points along the Natal and Transvaal borders, which were marked by the Thukela, Mzinyathi and Ncome rivers. He had originally intended all five columns to converge on the Zulu capital, Ulundi, but this plan resulted in a logistical nightmare which he lacked the facilities to resolve. In the end, only three of the columns were used offensively, the remaining two being intended to guard against Zulu counter-strikes.

The Right Flank Column (No. 1) was to cross into Zululand at the Lower Drift on the Thukela, under the command of Colonel C. K. Pearson, 3rd Buffs. No. 2 Column, under Colonel A. Durnford, R. E., was stationed in the difficult country above the Middle Drift of the Thukela. The Centre Column, No. 3., commanded by Colonel R. Glyn, 24th Regiment, was to cross into Zululand at Rorke's Drift on the Mzinyathi, while the Left Flank Column (No. 4), under Colonel H. E. Wood, VC, 90th L.I., would invade from a point known as Bemba's Kop on the Ncome. The remaining Column, No. 5, commanded by Colonel H. Rowlands, VC, was to be based at Luneburg in the Transvaal to keep an eye on both the Zulus and sullen republican elements in the Transvaal. Chelmsford himself accompanied the Centre Column.

The plan was essentially a sound one. The three invading columns were each thought to be

The First Invasion of Zululand, January to April 1879

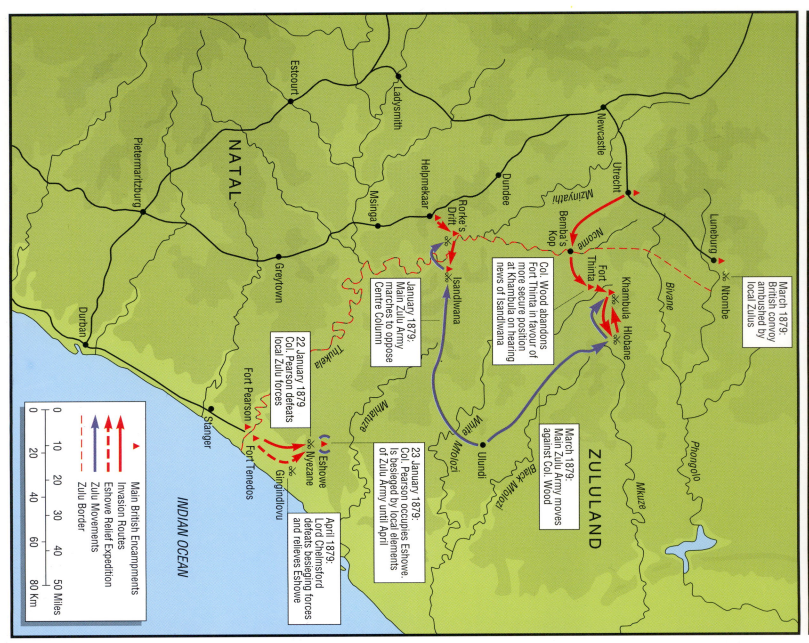

NATAL

Estcourt

Ladysmith

Pietermaritzburg

Helpmekaar

Dundee

Newcastle

Utrecht

Msinga

Greytown

Rorke's Drift

Bemba's Kop

Fort Thinta

Luneburg

Durban

Isandlwana

Khambula

Hlobane

ZULULAND

Stanger

Fort Pearson

Fort Tenedos

Eshowe

Nyezane

Gingindlovu

Ulundi

Ntombe

Bivane

Mkuze

Phongolo

Black Mfolozi

Mfolozi

White Mfolozi

Mhlatuze

Thukela

Mzinyathi

Ncome

INDIAN OCEAN

January 1879: Main Zulu Army marches to oppose Centre Column

Col. Wood abandons Fort Thinta in favour of more secure position at Khambula on hearing news of Isandlwana

22 January 1879: Col. Pearson defeats local Zulu forces

23 January 1879: Col. Pearson occupies Eshowe. Is besieged by local elements of Zulu Army until April

March 1879: Main Zulu Army moves against Col. Wood

March 1879: British convoy ambushed by local Zulus

April 1879: Lord Chelmsford defeats besieging forces and relieves Eshowe

Main British Encampments
Invasion Routes
Eshowe Relief Expedition
Zulu Movements
Zulu Border

0   10   20   30   40   50 Miles
0 20 40 60 80 Km

strong enough to defeat the Zulu army on its own, while the two reserve columns considerably reduced the risk of a Zulu raid against vulnerable settler communities. No message having been received from Cetshwayo by 11 January 1879, the columns began to cross into Zulu territory.

The Zulu Plan

King Cetshwayo had not wanted the war. Once British troops were on Zulu soil and attacking Zulu homesteads, his young warriors clamoured to be allowed to fight, but he forbade them to cross into Natal, hoping that a purely defensive war would win him political advantages.

The king correctly identified the Centre Column as the strongest among the invading forces. His strategy was to use warriors living in the country covered by the flanking columns to try to disrupt their advance, while the main Zulu Army was directed against the Centre Column. In

▲King Cetshwayo kaMpande. He became king in 1873, and attempted to revitalize the Zulu kingdom at a time when it was under threat from European encroachment. This brought him into conflict with the British and led to the disastrous Anglo-Zulu War of 1879. (Killie Campbell Collection)

the middle of January the king summoned the main army of more than 20,000 warriors to Ulundi. Cetshwayo did not take to the field himself, leaving command to his most senior general, Chief Ntshingwayo kaMahole Khoza, but in a final review he gave his warriors their overall instructions: he told them to march slowly and not tire themselves, and to avoid attacking entrenched positions. They were to drive the enemy back across the border, but on no account to follow them up. The great army marched off in high spirits, convinced of its invulnerability, and determined to wash its spears in the blood of the *abeLungu*, the White Men.

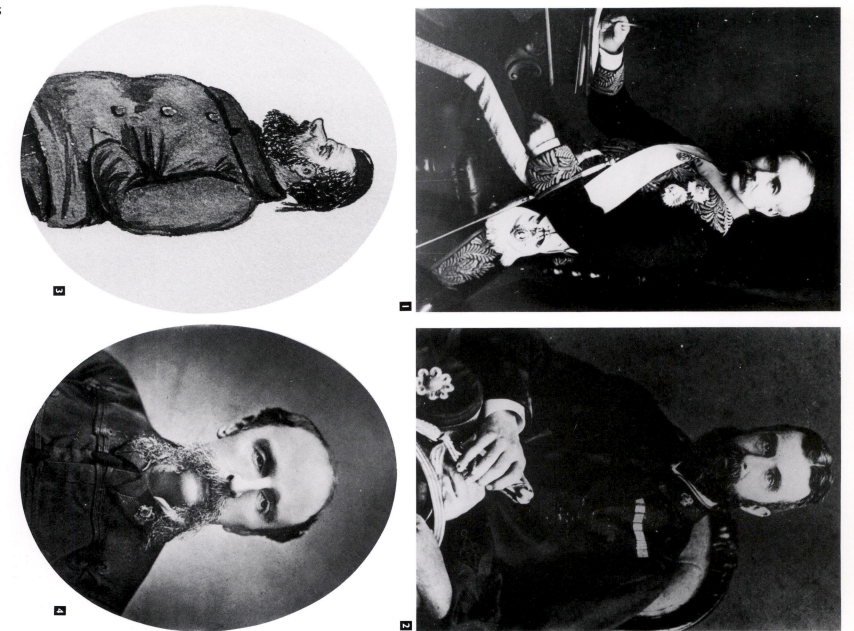

3

1

4

2

THE COMMANDERS

The British

The British commander, Lord Chelmsford, was in many ways a typical Victorian career soldier. He had joined the army in 1844, in time to see action in a number of Colonial campaigns. He had been present in Abyssinia in 1868, when the arid mountain landscape, the heat and thirst, and the insuperable problems of transport, had been as much the enemy as 'mad' King Theodore. He had also served in the Indian Mutiny, and when he succeeded Sir Arthur Cunynghame as Commander of British Forces in South Africa the Ninth Cape Frontier War, against the Xhosa people, was just drawing to a close. The Cape Frontier was a notoriously difficult theatre of operations, as the Xhosa traditionally employed elusive guerrilla tactics from wooded mountain strongholds or deep, bush-choked valleys. Chelmsford had a hotch-potch array of troops at his disposal, including local Volunteers, Irregulars, and African levies, stiffened by regular Imperial troops. With these he had successfully combed the bush and crushed the Xhosa. Chelmsford had earned some praise for the way he had handled his motley command, often under the most trying circumstances, but the lessons he learned seem to have left him ill-equipped for a war against the Zulus. He had seen rare Xhosa massed attacks collapse in the face of disciplined volley-fire, and he was convinced that African warriors could not sustain a heavy attack in the face of concentrated firepower. The impeccable manners of this tall, Victorian gentleman masked his lack of respect for the military capabilities of Colonials. Confidant that Imperial troops could win the day, he consistently disregarded the advice of those who knew the country and the Zulus. But the Zulus fought a different type of war from the Xhosa, and nothing in Chelmsford's experience had prepared him for it. His main worry, expressed on a number of occasions, was that he might have difficulty in bringing them to battle.

The campaign had not been long under way when Chelmsford ordered No. 2 Column, under the command of Colonel Anthony Durnford, R.E., up to support him. Durnford was a controversial character. He had been stationed in Natal for a number of years as the Colony's chief Engineer, and he admired and respected the black population. In 1873 he had been placed in command of a party of Volunteers who had been directed to stop Chief Langalibalele from fleeing across the Drakensberg mountains during a minor rebellion. Durnford had intercepted Langalibalele at Bushman's Pass, but in the ensuing skirmish was forced to retreat. Three Volunteers were killed and

1 *Sir Henry Bartle Edward Frere, the British High Commissioner for Southern Africa. Frere was charged with the introduction of a policy of Confederation, to facilitate British rule. He quickly became convinced that the Zulus were a major obstacle to the scheme. (S. Bourquin)*

2 *Lieutenant-General Frederic Thesiger, 2nd Baron Chelmsford. He was the senior British commander in South Africa. He was experienced in Colonial warfare, but underestimated the Zulu strength. (S. Bourquin)*

3 *Colonel Richard Glyn, 24th Regiment. Glyn was the commander of No. 3 Column, but Lord*

Chelmsford's decision to accompany the Column effectively took the command out of his hands. Glyn suggested the laagering of the camp at Isandlwana, but was over-ruled by Chelmsford. (National Army Museum)

4 *Brevet Colonel A. W. Durnford, RE, who commanded No. 2 Column. Durnford was an advocate of the use of black troops, and his own command largely consisted of Africans. Chelmsford considered him impetuous, and many have since blamed him for the Isandlwana disaster. (Ian Knight Collection)*

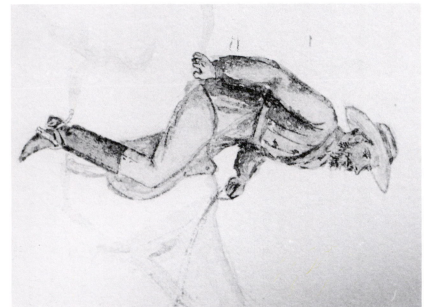

Durnford himself lost the use of his left arm, which thereafter he habitually wore thrust into the front of his tunic. Although Durnford's personal courage was never doubted, many considered the incident a fiasco, and held him to blame. At the outset of the Zulu campaign, Durnford had argued for a properly uniformed and organized force to be raised from among Natal's black population, most of whom were hostile to the Zulus. Lack of funds and Colonial nervousness had curtailed the raising of anything more than an unsophisticated Levy,

▲Colonel Henry Evelyn Wood, 90th Light Infantry, who commanded No. 4 Column. Wood was an energetic and capable officer with a flair for Colonial warfare. He wore this uniform throughout the Zulu War, apart from the helmet which he apparently replaced with a plain foreign service pattern. (Ian Knight Collection)

▼Lieutenant-Colonel Redvers Buller, Wood's dynamic cavalry commander. Wood was one of the few Imperial officers who realized the potential of locally raised irregular cavalry: this sketch shows the practical kit he wore in the field. (National Army Museum)

but Durnford's personal command was made up largely of black troops, who held him in high regard. His relationship with Chelmsford was strained, however, as Chelmsford considered him impetuous, and on one occasion had felt it necessary to censure him for disobeying orders and acting on his own initiative.

Of the remaining columns, the most important was the Left Flank Column, commanded by Colonel Henry Evelyn Wood. He, too, had seen a good deal of active service, and his interesting career was to take him from Midshipman in the Navy to Field Marshal in the Army! He had been a member of a group of promising officers gathered together by the *enfant terrible* of the military establishment, General Sir Garnet Wolseley, and known as the 'Ashanti Ring' after their service in West Africa in 1873. Wood was slightly vain and had a reputation for being accident-prone – he was once trampled by a giraffe – but he was a thorough and energetic officer with a rare flair for Colonial warfare, and he had served under Chelmsford on the Cape Frontier.

Wood's commander of cavalry, and very much

▲Chief Zibhebhu kaMapitha, a Zulu regimental commander and perhaps the most talented Zulu general of his generation. He fought at Isandlwana, where he was wounded in the hand, and later at Khambula and Ulundi. (S. Bourquin)

his right-hand man, was Lieutenant-Colonel Redvers Buller. He had seen action in China, and was another member of the 'Ashanti Ring'. He had commanded Irregulars on the Cape Frontier, and was one of the few Imperial officers to recognize their worth. He was a dynamic and charismatic leader, and a tough and tenacious fighter. His personal courage was legendary, and this, combined with his habitual care for his men's welfare, had earned him their devotion. In the coming campaign, Wood and Buller would prove a deadly combination.

The Zulus

Since, with the exception of Shaka, it was not customary for a Zulu king to command his army in person, it was left to his senior representatives to lead them into battle. In 1879 the main Zulu army was comanded by the Chiefs Mnyamana kaNgqengelele and Ntshingwayo kaMahole.

Chief Mnyamana was an immensely powerful figure. He was leader of the Buthelezi clan, one of the most important in the kingdom, and he had been Cetshwayo's principal *induna* since his coronation. As such, he was effectively the nation's prime minister, and it was in that capacity, rather than as a military commander, that he accompanied the army. He was in his mid-sixties, a tall, spare man with a peaked beard and greying hair, a deep voice and an imposing manner.

The man appointed to direct the troops was Chief Ntshingwayo kaMahole. He was also a man of great renown and considerable military ability, and he and Mnyamana were close personal friends. He was shorter and fatter than Mnyamana, but a greater orator.

There were a number of other talented commanders in the Zulu forces. Chief Zibhebhu kaMapitha was head of the Mandlakazi, a section of the Zulu Royal House, and a cousin of the king's. Again, he was a very powerful man within the kingdom, who had fostered close links with white traders, and grown wealthy as a result. In the prime of life, he was known to be discontented with his role as a provincial Chief. He had opposed the war, but once the fighting began he threw himself wholeheartedly into it. He was perhaps the most inspired Zulu tactician of his generation, but circumstances would remove him from the field for much of the war. The king's half-brother, Prince Dabulamanzi kaMpande, was another younger leader, reckless and headstrong, a fierce royalist and a supporter of the war. He was to be one of the few commanders to achieve reknown amongst the British, who attributed many deeds to him that had been performed by other commanders. Nevertheless, he was personally courageous, a good shot, and a daring leader.

There were other Zulu *indunas* who would distinguish themselves during the war, both high and low. Sigcwelegcwele kaMhlekehleke was the dynamic leader of the iNgobamakhosi, the largest and perhaps most aggressive of the younger regiments in the army. Serving as a junior commander in the same regiment was Mehlokazulu kaSihayo, who had been named by the British in the Ultimatum as one of those who had violated the Natal border. Like many of his generation, he resented European influence in Zulu affairs, and had no great respect for white culture or methods of fighting. And therein lay the great Zulu weakness: their commanders were able men who had grown up in an environment which had honoured the military virtues of courage and discipline, but very few of them had ever experienced the devastating effect of European firepower, and many of the younger warriors had not yet been tested in any battle.

▼ *Prince Dabulamanzi kaMpande, photographed after the end of the Zulu War. He commanded the uNdi corps during its unsuccessful attack against Rorke's Drift, and later fought in the Eshowe sector. (National Army Museum)*

▲ *Chief Sigcwelegcwele kaMhlekehleke, commander of the iNgobamakhosi ibutho. The iNgobamakhosi was one of the youngest regiments in the Zulu army and a favourite of the king's. It played a prominent part at Isandlwana, Khambula and Ulundi. Sigcwelegcwele himself fought at Isandlwana and Gingindlovu. (S. Bourquin)*

THE ARMIES: ISANDLWANA CAMPAIGN

Chelmsford's Centre Column

Chelmsford's No. 3 or Centre Column was both his strongest and his most experienced. Nominally it was under the command of Colonel Richard Glyn, 24th Regiment, but the presence of Chelmsford himself effectively reduced Glyn's role to that of a cipher. The Column's backbone consisted of the two battalions of the 24th Regiment (2nd Warwickshires). It was unusual for two infantry battalions of the same regiment to be serving together, because the reforms instituted by Minister of War Edward Cardwell, when introducing the system of two linked battalions, had intended that one should always remain at the home depot while the other served overseas. In fact, the demands of policing an expanding empire meant that at any given time more battalions were overseas than were at home. The 1/24th had been overseas for a number of years, and had been in South Africa since 1875. It had played a prominent part in the Cape Frontier War, and its massed rifle-fire had broken a Xhosa charge at the battle of Centane in February 1878. Each Imperial infantry battalion had a theoretical strength of eight companies of 100 men each, but sickness and detached duty meant that they were seldom up to strength. The 1/24th mustered less than 700 men, but most of its NCOs and many of the Other Ranks were long-service men, and the battalion as a whole was composed of mature, seasoned, acclimatized veterans who were used to serving together and with their officers.

The 2/24th, by contrast, had been raised under the recently introduced Short Service system – whereby a man enlisted for six years' active service, rather than twelve as before – and many had been recruited at Brecon, in South Wales, where the regimental depot had been established in 1873. As a result, most of its men were younger, and there was a higher proportion of Welsh accents. The 2nd Battalion had arrived in South Africa in 1878, and had been employed to mop up the last Xhosa resistance in the bush country. They were therefore less experienced than the men of their sister battalion, but were nonetheless fast becoming acclimatized to South African conditions. If there was any rivalry between the two battalions, it seems to have been friendly, and the officers were apparently delighted to be working together.

In 1879 the British Army was undergoing a period of increased professionalism. The long tradition of parade-ground manoeuvres and conspicuous uniforms was at last giving way to more fluid tactical theories and an appreciation of camouflage. None the less, British troops still went to war in Zululand wearing scarlet jackets, blue trousers and white foreign service helmets – one of the last major campaigns in which they did so. At the same time, half a world away, troops fighting in Afghanistan were wearing khaki. Each regiment was distinguished by coloured patches on the collar and cuffs, and by regimental badges on the collar and helmet. The 24th's facings were green, and their collar badge was a sphinx. Surprisingly, the red jacket was not always conspicuous in the sometimes harsh browns and greens of the African landscape, but the white helmet was a gleaming and tempting target. Veterans soon learned to remove the brass badge and tone down the helmet with dye improvised from tea, coffee or tree-bark.

Infantry equipment consisted of the integrated Valise Pattern system. This included a waist-belt with ammunition pouches on each side of the buckle, containing a total of forty rounds, and a black leather 'expense pouch' containing a further thirty rounds. A rolled greatcoat, mess-tin and the valise were supported by braces, although the

▲ *Gunner, Royal Artillery, Zulu War. Most RA other ranks seem to have prefered the undress frock coat on active service, rather than the more ornate tunic, while officers usually wore the braided dark blue patrol jacket.*

▲ The 1/24th in South Africa. This particular company remained on outpost duty in southern Natal during the Zulu War and so missed the disaster at Isandlwana. Nevertheless it presents an excellent picture of the mature veterans who made up the battalion. (RRW Museum, Brecon)

▲ The 1/24th on the march from the Cape Frontier, where they had played an active part in suppressing the Xhosa, to Zululand. The Irregulars seated on the right are probably from Buller's unit, the Frontier Light Horse. (Ian Knight Collection)

valise was usually carried in transport wagons on campaign. A wooden water-bottle over one shoulder, and a canvas haversack over the other, completed the equipment. Infantry weapons consisted of the 1871 pattern Martini–Henry rifle, a single-shot breech-loader which fired a heavy .450 bullet. It was sighted up to 1,450 yards, but its most effective battle range was 350 yards. It was topped by a socket bayonet which the troops nicknamed 'the lunger'.

Officers wore either a scarlet or blue braided patrol jacket, and carried swords and revolvers.

In addition to his infantry, Chelmsford had

N/5 Battery, Royal Artillery, which consisted of six 7pdr Rifled Muzzle-Loading guns. The 7pdr had originally been designed as a mountain gun, but its narrow carriage had proved unsuitable for South Africa, where it was mounted instead on 'Kaffrarian' carriages, modified versions of the larger 9pdr gun carriage. The 7pdr had a maximum range of 3,100 yards, but it suffered from a low muzzle velocity which reduced the effectiveness of shrapnel and shell. The Royal Artillery wore a blue uniform with yellow piping.

Chelmsford's force was singularly lacking in regular cavalry. To make up for this deficiency, several squadrons of Mounted Infantry had been raised. These consisted of men from Infantry Battalions who could ride. They wore their regimental jackets with buff cord riding-breeches, and were armed with Swinburne–Henry Carbines. They were augmented by men from the Natal Volunteer Corps. These were men from the Natal settler population, who had formed Volunteer units once it became clear that the British Government was not prepared to maintain a large garrison in the Colony during peacetime. The government provided uniforms and weapons, the men provided their own horses. The men knew the country and were often good riders and shots, but their numbers were small, and only the quasi-military Natal Mounted Police approached the disciplinary standards of regular troops. Most Volunteer units adopted black or blue uniforms with white helmets. The Centre Column included detachments of the Natal Mounted Police, Natal Carbineers, Buffalo Border Guard and Newcastle Mounted Rifles.

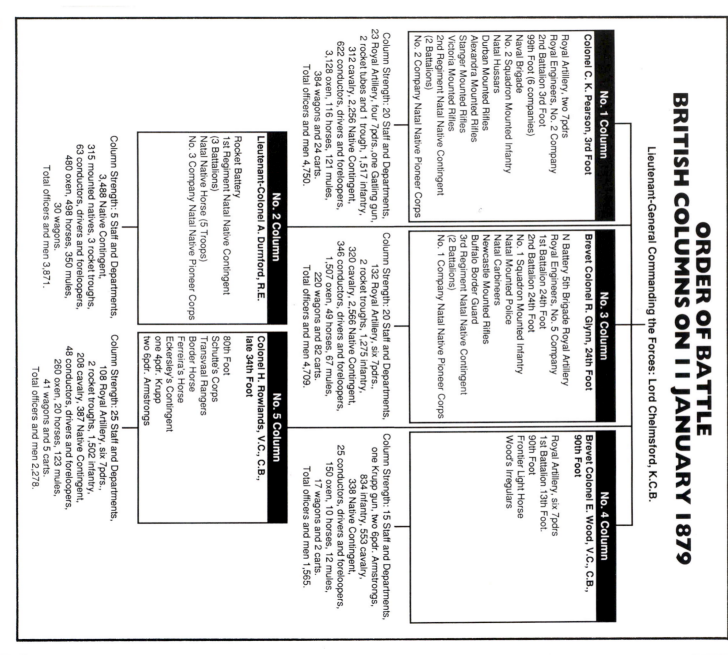

ORDER OF BATTLE
BRITISH COLUMNS ON 11 JANUARY 1879

Lieutenant-General Commanding the Forces: Lord Chelmsford, K.C.B.

No. 1 Column

Colonel C. K. Pearson, 3rd Foot

Royal Artillery, two 7pdrs
Royal Engineers, No. 2 Company
2nd Battalion 3rd Foot
99th Foot (6 companies)
Naval Brigade
No. 2 Squadron Mounted Infantry
Natal Hussars
Durban Mounted Rifles
Alexandra Mounted Rifles
Stanger Mounted Rifles
Victoria Mounted Rifles
2nd Regiment Natal Native Contingent (2 Battalions)
No. 2 Company Natal Native Pioneer Corps
Column Strength: 20 Staff and Departments, 23 Royal Artillery, four 7pdrs...one Gatling gun, 2 rocket tubes and 1 trough, 1,517 infantry, 312 cavalry, 2,256 Native Contingent, 622 conductors, drivers and foreloopers, 3,128 oxen, 116 horses, 121 mules, 384 wagons and 24 carts.
Total officers and men 4,750.

No. 3 Column

Brevet Colonel R. Glyn, 24th Foot

N Battery 5th Brigade Royal Artillery
Royal Engineers, No. 5 Company
2nd Battalion 24th Foot
No. 1 Squadron Mounted Infantry
Natal Mounted Police
Natal Carbineers
Newcastle Mounted Rifles
Buffalo Border Guard
3rd Regiment Natal Native Contingent (2 Battalions)
No. 1 Company Natal Native Pioneer Corps
Column Strength: 20 Staff and Departments, 132 Royal Artillery, six 7pdrs, 2 rocket troughs, 1,275 infantry, 320 cavalry, 2,566 Native Contingent, 346 conductors, drivers and foreloopers, 1,507 oxen, 49 horses, 67 mules, 220 wagons and 82 carts.
Total officers and men 4,709.

No. 4 Column

Brevet Colonel E. Wood, V.C., C.B.,

Royal Artillery, six 7pdrs
1st Battalion 13th Foot.
90th Foot
Frontier Light Horse
Wood's Irregulars
Column Strength: 15 Staff and Departments, one Krupp gun, two 6pdr. Armstrongs, 834 infantry, 553 cavalry, 338 Native Contingent, 25 conductors, drivers and foreloopers, 150 oxen, 10 horses, 12 mules, 17 wagons and 2 carts.
Total officers and men 1,565.

No. 2 Column

Lieutenant-Colonel A. Durnford, R.E.

Rocket Battery
1st Regiment Natal Native Contingent (3 Battalions)
Natal Native Horse (5 Troops)
No. 3 Company Natal Native Pioneer Corps
Column Strength: 5 Staff and Departments, 3,488 Native Contingent, 315 mounted natives, 3 rocket troughs, 63 conductors, drivers and foreloopers, 480 oxen, 498 horses, 350 mules, 30 wagons.
Total officers and men 3,871.

No. 5 Column

Colonel H. Rowlands, V.C., C.B., late 34th Foot

80th Foot
Schutte's Corps
Transvaal Rangers
Border Horse
Ferreira's Horse
Eckersley's Contingent
one 4pdr. Krupp
two 6pdr. Armstrongs
Column Strength: 25 Staff and Departments, 108 Royal Artillery, six 7pdrs, 2 rocket troughs, 1,502 infantry, 208 cavalry, 387 Native Contingent, 48 conductors, drivers and foreloopers, 260 oxen, 20 horses, 123 mules, 41 wagons and 5 carts.
Total officers and men 2,278.

Despite the opposition of a sector of the settler community, who were afraid that the arming of the Colony's black population might pose a threat to their security, Lord Chelmsford had raised several regiments of the Natal Native Contingent. Each consisted of two or three battalions, each of ten companies of nine white NCOs and 100 levies. The men were drawn from clans that had suffered heavily from Zulu raids in past generations. They were in plentiful supply and were highly motivated, but such potential as they might have had was largely squandered. Although some attempt was

A Sergeant of the 24th Regiment in full marching order. Those experienced in African warfare soon learned to remove their helmet plates and dull their helmets to a less conspicuous neutral brown colour with dyes improvised from tea or coffee. At Isandlwana the 24th would not have been wearing their valises and rolled greatcoats. (Mike Chappell)

made to appoint NNC officers from amongst the ranks of those who spoke Zulu, the NCOs were drawn from the dregs of Colonial society, and inspired no confidence in their men. Only one man in ten was issued with a firearm – usually of obsolete pattern – and only four rounds of ammunition: the rest carried traditional shields and spears. There were no uniforms available, and the men were distinguished by a red rag worn around the head, and by a few items of cast-off European clothing. Both battalions of the 3rd NCC accompanied the Central Column.

Early in the course of the war, Chelmsford ordered Durnford's No. 2 Column up from the Middle Drift to support his command. Durnford's force was almost entirely composed of black troops, including the 1st Battalion, 1st NNC. It also included five troops of mounted Africans, each of about fifty men, known collectively as the Natal Native Horse. Three of these troops were drawn from the amaNgwane, a Natal clan with a tradition of hostility to the Zulus, and known as the Sikhali Horse, after their Chief. One of the

▼Top: Members of Major Bengough's battalion of the Natal Native Contingent. These men carry their own shields and spears and are distinguished by a red headband. The N.N.C. were poorly armed, equipped and organized and their performance suffered accordingly. They have often been blamed – unfairly – for the disaster at Isandlwana. (Buffs Museum, Canterbury)

▼A British column on the march; the banks of a stream have had to be cut away to enable it to cross. The invasion of Zululand – a rugged country without roads – presented Chelmsford with a logistical nightmare. (Ian Knight Collection)

remaining troops consisted of Sotho horsemen under their Chief, Hlubi, who were old friends of Durnford's and had fought with him at Bushman's Pass. The final troop was drawn from the Christian Edendale Mission in Natal. The NNH men wore European clothing, with red rags wound around their wide-brimmed hats. Most preferred to ride bare-foot, but the Edendale men were booted and spurred. All were armed with carbines, and some carried spears in quivers over their shoulders or attached to their saddles.

Durnford's only Imperial troops consisted of three 9pdr Hales rocket troughs. Rockets were notoriously unreliable weapons, inaccurate, erratic in flight and unpredictable on impact, but they were considered useful in Colonial warfare, where their fearsome screech and the shower of sparks they gave off in flight was considered to have a tremendous psychological effect.

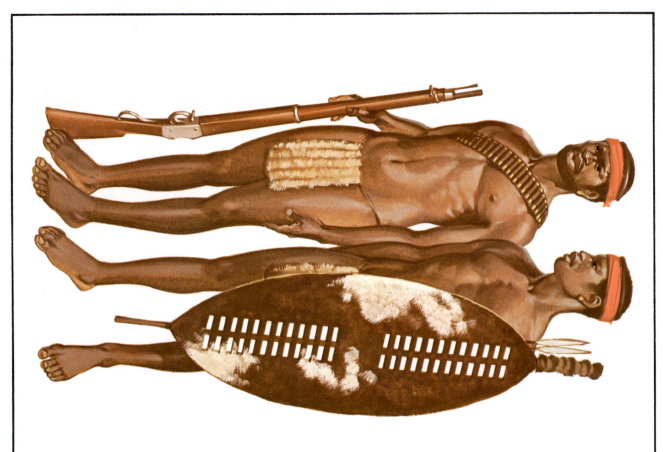

▶ *Two constables of the Natal Mounted Police, 1879. The N.M.P. was the most organized and disciplined of the Natal units. It wore black corduroy uniforms. (National Army Museum)*

▲ *The British forces recruited large numbers of African auxiliaries from the black population in Natal, which was historically antagonistic towards the Zulu kingdom. By and large, however, this potential asset was squandered as the resulting Natal Native Contingents were badly armed and poorly led. Only one in ten was issued with a firearm, and the rest fought with their own spears and shields. Their only uniform was a red rag around the head. (Angus McBride)*

▼ *The original caption of this photograph merely says 'Transport problems'; these oxen were struck down by a freak storm. A graphic illustration of the difficulties Chelmsford faced. (John Young Collection)*

Brevet Major Russell of 11/7 Battery RA, with

Of course, all of these units required considerable logistical support, and the transport situation remained a nightmare which tormented Chelmsford. Each infantry battalion needed to carry its own ammunition, tents, entrenching tools, signalling and medical equipment, and rations. On average, this amounted to seventeen wagon loads per battalion, without such luxuries as bottled beer and rum, and the officers' personal effects. There was a limited number of mule-drawn Army transport wagons available, but not nearly enough, and Chelmsford had to buy in civilian wagons at grossly inflated prices. These were large, heavy ox-wagons which, fully loaded, required as many as eighteen oxen to drag them. If they were to remain healthy, oxen needed up to sixteen hours' a day grazing and resting, or they dropped like flies. At best their progress might amount to about ten miles a day, and in bad weather, or across open country, or on roads damaged by erosion, it would be much less. Furthermore, Chelmsford had only a ludicrously small trained transport staff available, and had to make up the short-fall with volunteers, whose enthusiasm did not always compensate for their ineptitude. By the time hostilities began,

Chelmsford had amassed a total of 977 wagons, 56 carts, 10,023 oxen, 803 horses and 398 mules. The difficulties in managing such numbers can be easily imagined.

During the early stages of the war, too, there was a shortage of Royal Engineers, only one company – less than 200 officers and men – distributed throughout the entire column, and of medical staff, a handful of men of the Army Hospital Corps, augmented by volunteer civilian surgeons.

The Zulu Army

Unlike the British Army, the Zulu army was not a professional institution, but rather an armed citizenry. It was based on a system of age-grade regiments known as *amabutho* (sing. *ibutho*). Every few years the king would call together all youths throughout the country who had reached the age of eighteen or nineteen, and form them into an *ibutho*. They would be given a district where they built a barracks known as an *ikhanda*, which served as their headquarters. Each *ibutho* was given a distinctive name, and a uniform consisting of a

---

ORDER OF BATTLE
MAIN ZULU ARMY, 17 JANUARY 1879

Commander: Ntshingwayo kaMahole Khoza

uNdi Corps

Prince Dabulamanzi kaMpande
uThulwana (1,500)
iNdlondlo (900)
iNdluyengwe (1,000)

Amabutho unattached

Khandempemvu (umCijo) (2,500)
iNgobamakhosi (4,000)
uMbonambi (2,000)
uNokhenke (2,000)
uDloko (2,500)
uVe (2,000)

uNodwengu Corps

uDududu (1,500)
iMbube (500)
isAngqu (1,500)

NOTE: The British referred to *amabutho* who were based at the same *ikhanda* as a 'corps', hence 'uNdi Corps'. Unit strengths should be treated with caution, since the Zulus calculated strength not in complete regiments, but in the number of companies of a regiment present on a given occasion. Since the size of companies varied greatly, this is difficult to transpose into European terms. The strengths given here are rough estimates based on official British Intelligence counts before the war, and during the Isandlwana and Khambula campaigns. *Amabutho* which fought in the other theatres during the war have not been listed here, though elements from them may have fought with the main impi.

▲ A splendid study of a Zulu Chief in full regalia, photographed at the end of the nineteenth century. His body is almost totally obscured by cow-tails, and his head-dress consists of bunches of scarlet lourie and white ostrich feathers. This is typical of the ceremonial uniforms of the Zulu army in 1879, though most of it was not worn into battle. (Local History Museum, Durban)

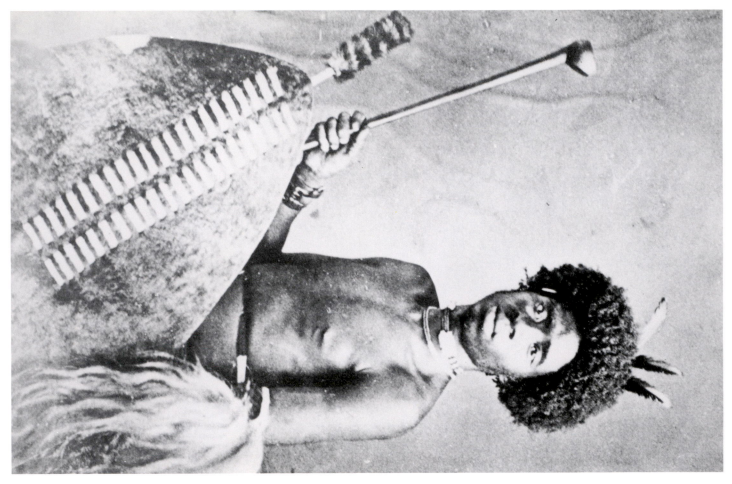

particular combination of feathers and furs, and a uniform shield-colour. They would remain in the king's service until he gave them permission to marry and disperse, at which point they passed from active service on to the national reserve list. Most warriors remained unmarried until their

thirties, and marriage signalled the point at which they transferred their first allegiance from the king to their own families. This artificial prolongation of bachelorhood had nothing to do with channelling sexual frustration into military aggression, as the British claimed; it was simply a means of

▲ *A young Zulu Warrior in 'war dress' – an abbreviated form of ceremonial dress – armed with a shield and knobkerry. This individual has frizzed his hair into an unusual style, a fashion among some young men in the 1870s. (Ian Knight Collection)*

▼ *Zulu warriors looting the camp in the aftermath of victory at Isandlwana. Religious custom dictated that the enemy dead be disembowelled, and the victorious warrior had to wear part of his victim's clothing until various cleansing ceremonies had been undertaken. All of these warriors are wearing war dress. The regiments are: 1, the Mbonambi, 2, the iNdlondlo and 3, the iNgobamakhosi. (Angus McBride)*

maximizing the period of national service, and in any case Zulu moral codes allowed for limited sexual activity outside marriage. In King Shaka's day, it was common for regiments to spend most of their time in the *amakhanda*, but by the 1870s the warriors lived mostly with their families, and only reported to their barracks when the king summoned them to perform a particular duty. When in service they were effectively the state labour-force; they tended the king's fields, took part in his hunts and the national ceremonies, policed his subjects and fought his wars.

In their military capacity, the *amabutho* functioned as battlefield tactical units. Each regiment was divided into two wings, right and left, and further sub-divided into companies of between fifty and seventy warriors apiece. Each company appointed its own leader from within its ranks, while wing commanders, the second-in-command and commander-in-chief were appointed by the king. Most *amabutho* were about 1,500 warriors strong, but some of the younger ones were much larger, reflecting Cetshwayo's success in revitalizing national institutions. The *amabutho* system fostered close ties between members of the same regiment, exaggerated by their common age and the fearsome reputation they enjoyed outside the kingdom. As a result, morale and *esprit de corps* was high, and rivalry between *amabutho* was common.

On ceremonial occasions each regiment wore a lavish uniform, but by 1879 very little of this was worn in battle, beyond perhaps a stuffed headband of animal-skin, and arm and leg ornaments made from the bushy part of cows' tails. Everyday dress consisted of a thin belt of hide around the waist, with strips of fur hanging at the front, and a square of softened cowhide over the buttocks.

Weapons consisted of a large oval cowhide war-shield, and a selection of spears. In Shaka's day the war shields were fully five feet high by almost three feet wide, but by 1879 a smaller variant, about 3.5 feet high by 2 feet wide, was more popular. War-shields were not the property of individual warriors, but were kept in special stores in the *amakhanda*. The hides were carefully matched for each regiment. Young regiments carried black shields; senior, usually married, regiments carried white or red shields. New

shields seem to have been issued periodically in any case Zulu moral codes allowed for limited regiment's lifespan, and the quantity and arrangement of white spots on a shield reflected its status.

The standard Zulu weapon remained the stabbing spear, apparently introduced by Shaka. This had a blade between 12 and 18 inches long, mounted in a stout haft, and was used with a powerful under-arm thrust. In addition, many warriors carried lighter spears, with smaller blades, which were used for throwing. These could be flung with some accuracy up to a maximum of fifty yards.

By 1879, the Zulu army had also acquired large numbers of firearms. King Cetshwayo's white adviser, John Dunn, had imported a number into the kingdom, and many more came in through Portuguese Mozambique in the north, or illegally across the Natal border. British observers were shocked to see that most warriors could lay their hands on some firearm or other, but most were obsolete percussion models or old Brown Bess types, usually in poor condition. With no training, regular ammunition supplies or spare parts, the Zulus were unable to make the most of their firepower, but subsequent reports stress its volume, and it was to boast a number of notable successes.

Unlike the British, the Zulu army was highly mobile, and required no baggage train. It normally could march twenty miles in a day, and twice that distance was not unknown. For the first few days it would be accompanied by civilians – usually boys too young to fight – who drove slaughter cattle and carried corn and beer. After that, it was expected to live by foraging. In Shaka's time, this was usually enough to see it beyond the kingdom's borders, but in 1879 it was fighting on home territory, which led to problems with provisions and a tension within the civilian population, whose crops were likely to suffer on the army's approach.

Tactically, the army was wedded to an aggressive manoeuvre known as 'the beast's horns'. One formation, usually of senior warriors, and called 'the chest', would advance straight at the enemy, while on each side younger regiments, known as 'the horns', would rush out to surround him. The Zulus were able to perform this tactic in close formation, moving at great speed over broken

▲ *Zulu warriors in action in 1879. This illustration gives a good impression of their appearance in the field. They have discarded their ceremonial regalia, retaining only a few plumes. Note the number of firearms. (Ian Knight Collection)*

▲ *The Zulu attack formation was called impondo zankomo, the 'beast's horns'. The centre, or 'chest', made a frontal assault on the enemy while the 'horns' rushed out to surround it on each side. (S Bourquin)*

ground, as Chelmsford would soon discover to his cost.

The great army which left Ulundi consisted of twelve full regiments: the uDududu, isAngqu, iMbube, uNokhenke, Khandempemvu (umCijo), uMbonambi, iNgobamakhosi, uVe, uThulwana, iNdluyengwe, iNdlondlo and uDloko, augmented by small detachments from regiments that were fighting elsewhere. Several were regiments of married men, recalled to active duty at this time of national trial, but the majority were young un-married warriors in their prime.

THE FIRST PHASE OF THE WAR

Chelmsford's orders to Pearson's No. 1 Column were to advance north from the Lower Drift to the abandoned mission station of Eshowe, some 35 miles from the border. Because this had a number of buildings which could be used as stores, it had been selected as the most suitable base for future operations. After several days spent ferrying supplies across the Thukela, Pearson began his advance on 18 January. He had just crossed the Nyezane river on the 22nd when he was attacked in the open by a force of about 6,000 Zulus. Heavy fighting lasted for about an hour and a half before the Zulus were defeated. Pearson, who lost ten men killed and sixteen wounded, immediately pushed on to Eshowe which he reached the following day. Once in position he began to fortify the deserted mission.

Wood's No. 4 Column had not been allocated an immediate strategic objective, but was required to subdue the northern reaches of the Zulu kingdom. The area was home to a number of aggressive and semi-independent Zulu groups, including followers of the renegade Swazi prince Mbilini, and the abaQulusi, who were descendants of an *ibutho* established by Shaka, who had settled in the area. The Zulus operated from a chain of flat-topped mountain strongholds, Zungwini, Hlobane and Ityenka. Wood immediately organized a series of far-ranging patrols to harry the Zulus. It was during a skirmish near Hlobane on 24 January that he received a message from Lord Chelmsford telling him that the Centre Column had suffered a major set-back.

The Advance to Isandlwana

Lord Chelmsford crossed the Mzinyathi river into Zululand at Rorke's Drift early on the morning of 11 January. The Royal Artillery covered the crossing from the Natal bank while a line of vedettes from the Natal Volunteers were the first across. One company of the 2/24th was left at Rorke's Drift to guard the supply depot and river crossing. Once the column was across, a new camp sprang up on the far bank, and the exhausting task of ferrying over the transport wagons began. There was no sign of the enemy.

Chelmsford intended to establish his first base inside enemy territory at Isiphezi mountain, but first he had a local problem to resolve. A few miles ahead along the line of his advance the track cut across a stream known as the Batshe, close to the homestead of an important Zulu Chief named Sihayo. His sons had been responsible for one of the border incidents that had provoked the war, and in any case Chelmsford could not afford to leave a potentially hostile force in his rear. Accordingly, on 12 January he undertook an attack on Sihayo's stronghold, which was in a gorge set into a line of cliffs overlooking the eastern bank of the Batshe. Sihayo and many of his men were absent at Ulundi, having attended the general muster, but a small force had been left to guard his homestead. Chelmsford's attacking force comprised four companies of the 2/24th, the 3rd N.N.C. and the mounted troops. The N.N.C. were instructed to carry out a frontal assault which, with some encouragement, they succeeded in doing. A line of 24th men followed them with fixed bayonets. The mounted men and the remainder of the infantry surrounded the stronghold by climbing the cliffs on either side, and the position was taken after a stiff skirmish which claimed the lives of about thirty Zulus. Chelmsford ordered Sihayo's homestead to be burnt and, having rounded up the Chief's cattle, the British returned to camp.

With this threat removed, Chelmsford was free to turn his attention once more to his advance. His route lay across country that was alternately rocky

The Isandlwana Campaign, 11 to 23 January 1879

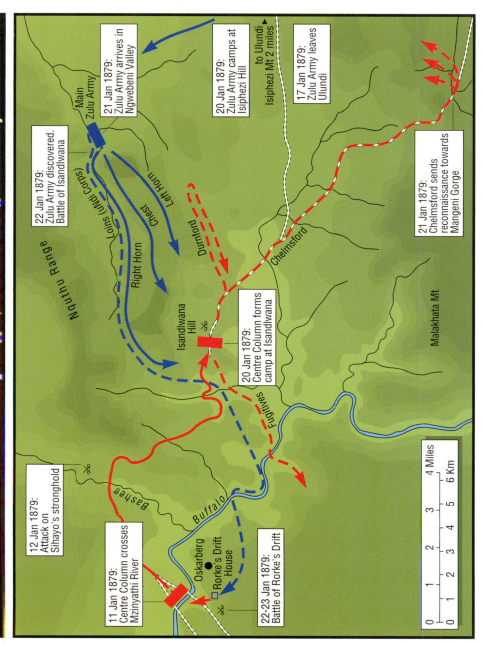

22 Jan 1879: Zulu Army discovered. Battle of Isandlwana

21 Jan 1879: Zulu Army arrives in Ngwebeni Valley

20 Jan 1879: Zulu Army camps at Isiphezi Hill

to Ulundi: Isiphezi Mt 2 miles

17 Jan 1879: Zulu Army leaves Ulundi

21 Jan 1879: Chelmsford sends reconnaissance towards Mangeni Gorge

20 Jan 1879: Centre Column forms camp at Isandlwana

12 Jan 1879: Attack on Sihayo's stronghold

11 Jan 1879: Centre Column crosses Mzinyathi River

22-23 Jan 1879: Battle of Rorke's Drift

Main Zulu Army

Loins (uNdi Corps)

Right Horn

Crest

Left Horn

Durnford

Chelmsford

Fugitives

Isandlwana Hill

Nquthu Range

Malakhata Mt

Bashee

Buffalo

Oskarberg

Rorke's Drift House

4 Miles

6 Km

and marshy, and which would therefore be very difficult for his transport wagons. It was necessary for Engineer parties to clear and repair the track, and while this work was going on, Chelmsford moved his camp to the ridge on the western bank of the Batshe. From here his scouts reported that the best place for his next camp site would be the eastern foot of a mountain known as Isandlwana.

At about this time, Chelmsford sent orders to Colonel Durnford, in command of No. 2 Column, instructing him to leave two battalions of his N.N.C. to guard the Middle Drift, to send one to the border magistracy at Msinga, and to move the rest of his forces up to Rorke's Drift. Chelmsford wanted Durnford on hand should he be needed to support the advance, and Durnford was delighted at the prospect of a more active role in the campaign. He arrived at Rorke's Drift on the 20th,

just as Chelmsford was pushing on to Isandlwana.

The track crested a rising nek which lay between Isandlwana mountain on the left and a stony kopjie on the right, then wound its way towards Isiphezi, and ultimately Ulundi, but Chelmsford's troops spilled off on either side, and at about noon began pitching their tents. Their camp was arranged in blocks running north to south along the base of the mountain; first the 2/3rd N.N.C., then the 1/3rd N.N.C., then the 2/24th, the Royal Artillery, mounted troops, and finally, south of the track below the stony kopjie, the 1/24th.

Throughout this time, Chelmsford had only the vaguest knowledge of the Zulu movements. The main *impi* had left Ulundi on 17 January and, following its orders, moved slowly towards the Centre Column. On the 20th it camped just north

▲ *Lieutenant-Colonel H. B. Pulleine, 24th Regiment. He was left in command of the camp at Isandlwana, with orders to defend it. His ability to do*

so was compromised by the need to support Durnford, once the latter had run into difficulties. (Ian Knight Collection)

The Battle of Isandlwana

Before the invasion had begun, Chelmsford had issued detailed regulations for the defence of all camps on the line of march, calling for wagon laagers or earth entrenchments at every stop. But when Colonel Glyn suggested protecting the camp at Isandlwana, Chelmsford himself decided

of Isiphezi hill, and on the following day it moved into the Nquthu hills north-east of Isandlwana. Here they rested in the valley of the Ngwebeni stream, about four miles from Isandlwana. They intended to remain there throughout the 22nd, because a new moon was imminent, and the night of a 'dead' moon was considered too ill an omen for so great an undertaking as an attack on a British camp.

Chelmsford received this note early on the morning of the 22nd and it took him by surprise; he had not expected Dartnell to engage the enemy, and now it appeared he had blundered into part of the main *impi*. Chelmsford decided that Dartnell and Lonsdale would not be strong enough to engage the *impi* alone, and he assembled a force to march to their relief. At about 4.00 a.m. he rode out of the camp with six companies of the 2/24th, four R.A. guns, a mounted infantry detachment, and the Natal Native Pioneers, heading for Mangeni.

The camp at Isandlwana was left in the hands of Lieutenant-Colonel Henry Pulleine, 1/24th, and the force at his disposal was still impressive: five companies of the 1/24th, one of the 2/24th, the two remaining 7pdr guns of N/5 Battery, more than a hundred mounted men from the Mounted Infantry and Natal Volunteers, and four companies of the N.N.C. Chelmsford's orders to Pulleine were that he should keep his cavalry vedettes advanced, draw in his line of infantry outposts, and

against it. The ground was too stony for a proper entrenchment, he considered it only a temporary halt, and the wagons had to be free to keep up the flow of supplies between the camp and Rorke's Drift. Chelmsford intended to move on as soon as possible, and no sooner had he arrived on the 20th than he set off on a reconnaissance towards the Mangeni gorge, about twelve miles eastwards. This was the stronghold of a Chief named Matshana, and the General ordered that the hills that flanked his planned advance should be thoroughly searched for signs of the enemy.

Accordingly, early on the morning of 21 January, Commandant Rupert Lonsdale left camp with sixteen companies of the 3rd N.N.C., followed by Major John Dartnell with a party of Natal Mounted Police and Volunteers. At the far end of the range, where it overlooked the Mangeni, Dartnell encountered more than 1,000 Zulus blocking any further advance. As darkness fell Dartnell decided to make camp for the night, though neither his nor Lonsdale's men had tents or supplies. A note was sent back to Chelmsford asking for reinforcements so that an attack could be made in the morning, and the force settled down for an uneasy night.

defend the camp if attacked. Before leaving, he also sent orders to Durnford at Rorke's Drift, ordering him to move his column up to Isandlwana, and informing him of his (Chelmsford's) movements. Once Durnford reached Isandlwana, there would be a total of 67 officers and 1,707 men in the camp to carry out the General's orders.

After Chelmsford marched out, Pulleine organized his defensive arrangements. The mounted men were deployed as vedettes on the Nquthu plateau and towards the east of the camp, where some were posted on a conical kopjie about a mile away. A screen of infantry pickets was placed about 1,500 yards from the camp, in a curve which stretched from the right in the south, round to a lip of the Nquthu plateau in the north. This commanded a spur where the ground sloped down to join the tail of Mount Isandlwana itself.

Shortly after 8.00 a.m. a mounted vedette rode into camp with the news that a large body of Zulus was approaching across the plateau from the north-east. The 'Fall In' was sounded, the infantry pickets came in (except for an N.N.C. outpost on the lip of the plateau), and the whole force formed up in front of the tents. Pulleine sent a note to Chelmsford informing him that the Zulus were approaching the camp in force. No further developments were reported by the vedettes until a message was delivered over an hour later, which stated that the Zulus had divided into three

▼ *A small diorama of the battlefield is dwarfed by the real Isandlwana behind. The great black arc on the model represents the Zulu*

attack: the numbers are perhaps exaggerated, but it does convey the overwhelming strength of the Zulu army. (Ian Knight Collection)

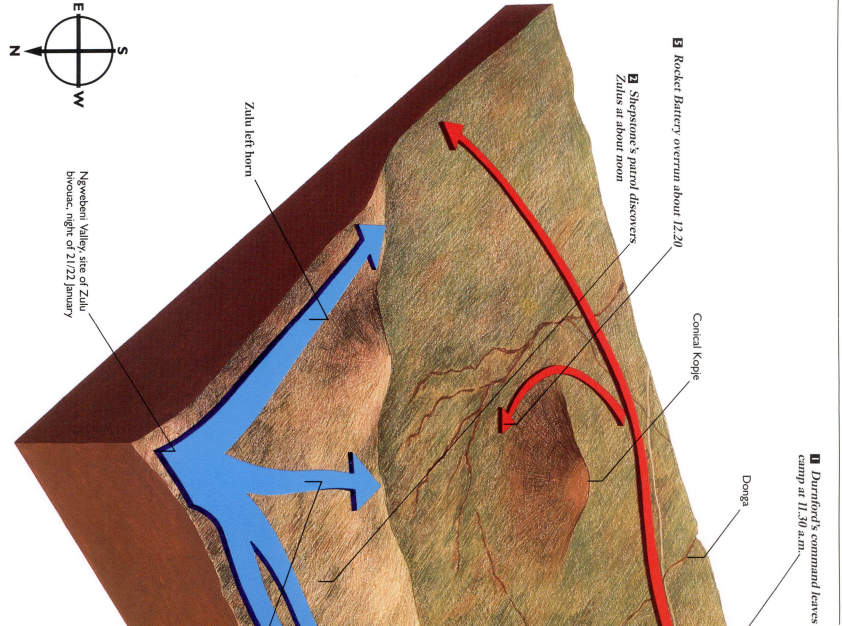

5 *Rocket Battery overrun about 12.20*

2 *Shepstone's patrol discovers Zulus at about noon*

Zulu left horn

Ngwebeni Valley, site of Zulu bivouac, night of 21/22 January

Conical Kopie

Donga

1 *Durnford's command leaves camp at 11.30 a.m.*

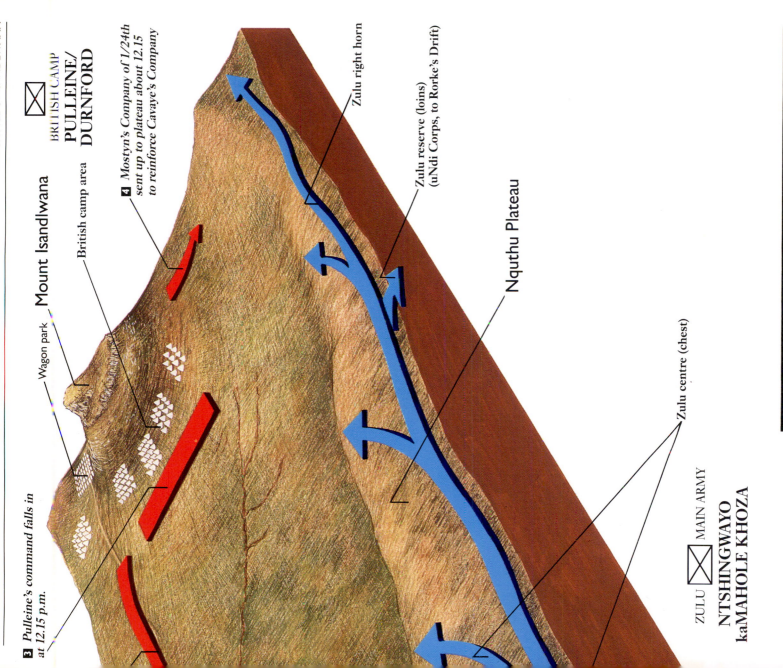

3 Pulleine's command falls in at 12.15 p.m.

4 Mostyn's Company of 1/24th sent up to plateau about 12.15 to reinforce Cavaye's Company

⊠ BRITISH CAMP
PULLEINE/ DURNFORD

Mount Isandlwana

British camp area

Wagon park

Zulu right horn

Zulu reserve (loins) (uNdi Corps, to Rorke's Drift)

Nquthu Plateau

Zulu centre (chest)

ZULU ⊠ MAIN ARMY
NTSHINGWAYO kaMAHOLE KHOZA

THE BATTLE OF ISANDLWANA
The Zulu approach and Durnford's sortie, to 12.20 p.m., 22 January 1879

columns. Two retired to the north until they were lost from sight, while the other was even then moving north-west. This report had just come in when Durnford rode into the camp with his men. Pulleine informed Durnford of the situation.

Chelmsford's orders to Durnford had not told him what to do on arriving at the camp, and this created an awkward situation. He had presumably been brought up to reinforce the camp, but he felt that he was also to support the advance if necessary. Durnford was senior to Pulleine and so normal military procedure would mean that he now commanded the camp, but it is unlikely that Chelmsford had had this in mind since he expected the camp to be moved forward to join him shortly. In the circumstances, Durnford felt able to act independently. The sound of gunfire had been heard at Mangeni and this, coupled with news of the Zulu movements on the hills, suggested that Chelmsford was engaged with the main *impi*. Durnford was worried that the Zulus spotted by the vedettes were moving off to threaten Chelmsford's rear. He felt that it was essential to

counter this, and ordered two troops of the N.N.H., under Captain George Shepstone, up on to the plateau to drive any Zulus they encountered to the east. Durnford himself proposed to move out across the plain with the remainder of his column to cut the Zulus off. He asked Pulleine to give him two companies of the 24th, but Pulleine, mindful of his specific orders to defend the camp, refused. Durnford accepted the situation and the two parted amicably, Durnford commenting that he would none the less expect to be supported if he got into difficulties.

Pulleine sent up a company of the 1/24th under Lieutenant Cavaye to support the N.N.C. picket on the head of the spur. Cavaye detached a platoon under Lieutenant Dyson to a point 500 yards farther to their left, where it could watch the rear approaches to Isandlwana. At about 11.30

a.m. Durnford rode out of Isandlwana, while his detached party fanned out to scout the plateau. About four miles from the camp, some of Lieutenant Raw's N.N.H. spotted a herd of cattle being driven by some Zulus, and they immediately gave chase. The herders promptly disappeared over a fold in the ground. Raw's men galloped up to the edge, then desperately reined in their horses. Dropping sharply away in front of them was the deep valley of the Ngwebeni, and below them, not miles away at Mangeni as they had thought, lay the 20,000 warriors of the main *impi*.

They were resting in silence, but the sight of British troops looking down on them was too much for the warriors, who, led by the nearest regiment, the Khandempemvu, immediately sprang up and began to clamber up the slopes towards the retreating horsemen. The senior *indunas* were powerless to stop them, and the regiments instinctively formed up in the traditional 'chest and horns' formation. The Khandempemvu and elements of the uMxhapo formed the chest, the uMbonambi, iNgobamakhosi and uVe the left horn, and the uDududu, iMbube, isAngqu and uNokhenke the right horn. Only the uNdi corps, consisting of the uThulwana, iNdluyengwe, iNdlondlo and uDloko regiments, were intercepted by the commanders and formed into the 'loins', or tactical reserve.

Raw's troop fell back, firing as they went. They met Shepstone, who sent a message to Durnford warning him of the Zulu approach, and then rode to pass the news to Pulleine himself. While Shepstone was delivering the message a note arrived from Lord Chelmsford, telling Pulleine to strike the tents and send on the baggage to join him. Pulleine, still not grasping the seriousness of the Zulu threat, merely sent back a note saying that he was unable to move the camp 'at present'. He sounded the 'Fall In' again and sent a second company, Captain Mostyn's, up to the plateau to reinforce Cavaye.

Durnford was advancing across the plain, below the Nquthu escarpment, when Shepstone's messenger reached him. He had no sooner halted his men than elements of the left horn appeared in strength on the rim of the plateau above. Durnford's men began to retire, halting every so

often to loose a volley. Meanwhile, Durnford's rocket battery and its escort, commanded by Major Russell, which was not mounted, had lagged behind. It had just passed the conical Kopje when news reached it of the Zulu approach. Russell turned to his left to climb the slope, but was stopped in his tracks by the sudden appearance of warriors on the skyline. Russell's men hastily set up their troughs, but had only managed to loose one salvo when a Zulu volley crashed down into them, causing the N.N.C. to flee. The Zulus then charged down and overran the battery. Russell was killed, but miraculously three of his men survived and escaped to safety.

As Mostyn's men reached the top of the spur they were greeted with a chilling sight. A massive column of Zulus, the right horn, was streaming across Cavaye's front at about 600 yards' distance. They were heading towards the rear of Isandlwana, and they took not the slightest notice of the fire Cavaye was directing at them. Mostyn placed his men between Cavaye and Dyson, and they joined in the shooting. At about this time, too, Shepstone's two troops of the N.N.H., who had been retiring in front of the Zulus, joined them on the spur. The N.N.C picket meanwhile had fallen back to the plain below.

Pulleine was still unaware of the extent of the attack, until more and more warriors began to appear on the skyline. Since that was obviously the direction of the main threat, he ordered Major Stuart Smith, RA to position his two 7pdrs on a low rocky knoll about 600 yards to the front of the camp. Here they opened fire on the Zulus spilling over the lip of the plateau. To support the guns, Lieutenant Porteus' company, 1/24th, formed up to their left, and Captain Wardell's company to the right. Lieutenant Pope's sole company of the 2/24th, which had been out on picket duty, was also on the plain in front of the camp, and took up a position facing the hills. The men were able to take advantage of the cover provided by a line of boulders which marked the point where the ground fell away towards a donga, or run-off gulley. Pulleine realised that he could not leave Mostyn and Cavaye exposed on the plateau, so he recalled them, and sent his last company of the 24th, Captain Younghusband's, to cover their

retreat. The N.N.H. and N.N.C. picket formed up on Younghusband's right, while Mostyn and Cavaye fell in line with Porteous. The infantry therefore formed a more or less continuous line from Younghusband on the left, stretching to Pope on the right, though they were spread dangerously thin. Exactly where the rest of the N.N.C. were no one is sure; one company was formed up in front of the camp itself; the rest seem to have been out on the right.

Durnford's men continued their retreat, picking up a vedette of the Natal Carbineers along the way. At about a mile from the camp they stopped in a deep donga and dismounted to open fire on their pursuers. Here they were joined by some of the mounted men from the camp. This placed Pulleine in a quandry. He remembered his promise to support Durnford if he got into difficulties, and sure enough Durnford was now under pressure way out to the right. Pulleine ordered Pope to fall back to direct some of his fire against the left horn facing Durnford, and the N.N.C. apparently filled the gap between them. The 24th were 'old, steady shots', but they were too scattered to concentrate their fire. Nevertheless they managed to slow the Zulu advance which stalled under the cover of a slight depression about 300 yards from the line. The frustrated Zulus, unable to move forward in the face of so murderous a fire, could be heard murmuring like a swarm of angry bees.

Durnford's men had been in action for some time now and were beginning to run out of ammunition. Attempts to resupply them were hampered by the fact that their runners could not find their own ammunition wagons, and the infantry quartermasters would not issue ammunition to Levies. Sensing the reduction in firepower, the iNgobamakhosi and uVe began to extend to their left, to outflank Durnford, and cross the donga farther down. Pulleine, aware of this, tried to counter it by having Smith turn his fire on the left horn. The climax of the battle had

▼Isandlwana battlefield, with the donga defended by Durnford in the foreground. Outflanked and running out of ammunition, Durnford retreated closer to the camp at the climax of the battle, allowing the Zulus to burst through the line. (Ian Knight Collection)

approached, and suddenly the tide turned against the British. Durnford's position was critical and he could no longer hold the donga. He ordered his men to mount up and ride back to the camp. It was probably at this point that the N.N.C., seeing them go, threw down their weapons and fled to the rear. In a few minutes the situation had become desperate. Pope was hopelessly exposed, and

▲This late Victorian engraving portrays the 24th as an island swamped by the tide of the Zulu advance. Although it exaggerates the size of the Zulu impi, it does suggest something of the way the regulars were overwhelmed as they tried to retreat towards the camp. (Ian Knight Collection)

▲The position occupied by the 24th companies at Isandlwana, looking towards Durnford's donga (marked by the white building in the distance). The boulders provided some cover, but the men were too thin on the ground to hold such a wide front. (Ian Knight Collection)

▲Inset: Lieutenant C. Pope, who commanded the only company of the 2/24th present at Isandlwana during the battle. His men held the right of the firing line and were outflanked when Durnford's men withdrew. Pope was killed in the battle. (Ian Knight Collection)

Pulleine tried frantically to pull his men back to a closer defensive position with the mountain at his back. The bugles sounded the retire, and the infantry stopped firing and began to fall back.

It was too late. An *induna* who had been observing the battle goaded the Khandempemvu in the centre into action, and, released from the galling fire, they rose and surged forward. The

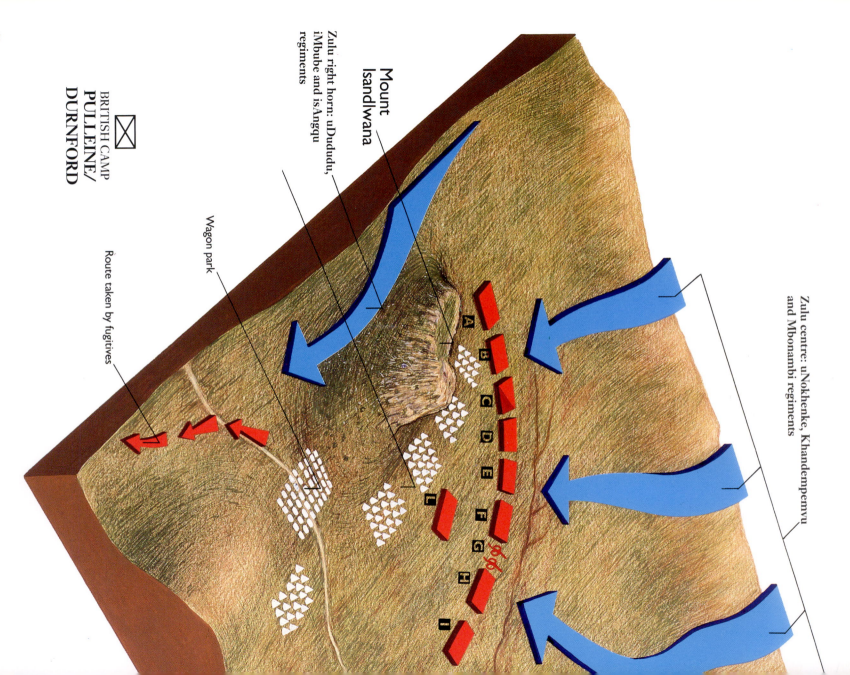

BRITISH CAMP
PULLEINE/
DURNFORD

Zulu right horn: uDududu,
iMbube and isAngqu
regiments

Mount
Isandlwana

Wagon park

Route taken by fugitives

Zulu centre: uNokhenke, Khandempemvu
and Mbonambi regiments

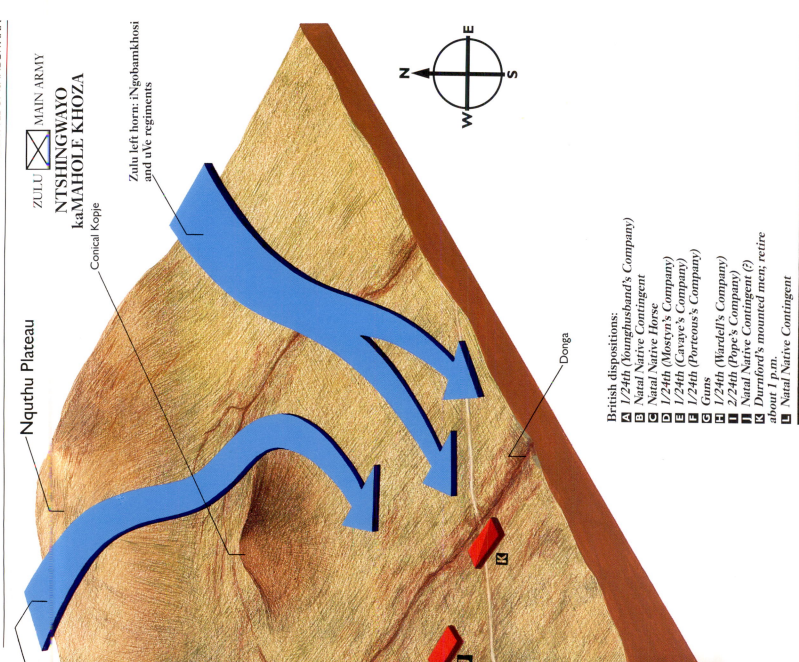

ZULU ⊠ MAIN ARMY

**NTSHINGWAYO
kaMAHOLE KHOZA**

Zulu left horn: iNgobamkhosi
and uVe regiments

Conical Kopje

Nquthu Plateau

Donga

British dispositions:

A *1/24th (Younghusband's Company)*
B *Natal Native Contingent*
C *Natal Native Horse*
D *1/24th (Mostyn's Company)*
E *1/24th (Cavaye's Company)*
F *1/24th (Porteous's Company)*
G *Guns*
H *1/24th (Wardell's Company)*
I *2/24th (Pope's Company)*
J *Natal Native Contingent (?)*
K *Durnford's mounted men; retire
   about 1 p.m.*
L *Natal Native Contingent*

THE BATTLE OF ISANDLWANA
The climax of the battle, about 1 p.m., 22 January 1879

▶A rather romanticized view of Isandlwana. In fact, the 24th companies did not take up such a tight formation, and this was the reason for their downfall: nevertheless, the picture does suggest the fierce nature of the hand-to-hand fighting. (Ian Knight Collection)

▶Below: C. E. Fripp's classic painting of the last moments of the 24th at Isandlwana. In fact, there was no Regimental Colour present in the firing line, but the picture is otherwise accurate. (National Army Museum)

▶The two 7pdr guns of N/5 Battery, RA, which were captured by the Zulus at Isandlwana. At the end of the war they were found abandoned on the veld near Ulundi. The Zulus had tried unsuccessfully to make them work. (Ian Knight Collection)

▶Brevet Major S. Smith., RA, who commanded the two guns at Isandlwana. Smith kept them firing for as long as possible, then tried to save them, but the guns became stuck in rough ground and were overrun. Smith himself was killed near the Fugitives' Drift.

regiments on either side followed them, and suddenly the entire *impi* was in motion once more. The 7pdrs kept firing until the last minute, then limbered up and careered back towards the camp. One gunner was stabbed to death as he mounted the axle-tree. The infantry grouped together in rallying squares, but the Zulus rushed in right amongst them, and pushed them back through the camp. It was no longer possible to make any concerted defence. Men stood back to back or in small clusters, firing until their ammunition was spent, then keeping the Zulus at bay with the bayonet. Individuals took refuge in and around the wagons, lashing about them with rifle butt and bayonet. Durnford dismissed the N.N.H. men who had fought well under his command, and gave them permission to leave the camp. Together with a mixed group of Volunteers and 24th men he took up a position just below the nek, trying to hold back the left horn. Here he was killed. Pulleine, too, died somewhere in the camp, and knots of the 24th held out in the broken ground behind Isandlwana, until the Zulus overwhelmed them. The Zulu horns had closed, and the battle was over.

Those who had managed to escape the carnage in the camp crossed the nek hoping to ride to Rorke's Drift, but were horrified to find that the right horn had already blocked their route. They veered to the left, down-valley of a stream known

49

▼The closing stages of Isandlwana: the firing line has collapsed, and the British infantry are pushed back into the camp, where much of the hand-to-hand fighting takes place. The two Zulus 1 are both of the uVe ibutho, the youngest in the Zulu army. They are wearing war-dress rather than full ceremonial regalia, although it is possible that more regalia was worn at Isandlwana than in later campaigns. The warrior on the right wears his hair fashionably styled with wax. 2 is an officer of the 24th, wearing the blue infantry-pattern patrol jacket, while 3 is a private with three 'long service and good conduct' chevrons, reflecting the seniority of many men in the 1st Battalion's ranks. (Angus McBride)

▲'The Pride of the 24th'; scattered infantry try to rally together as the Zulus overrun the line. A modern painting of the scene, by American artist Bud Bradshaw. (By Kind Permission of the Artist)

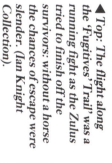

▲ Top: The flight along
the 'Fugitives' Trail' was a
running fight as the Zulus
tried to finish off the
survivors: without a horse
the chances of escape were
slender. (Ian Knight
Collection).

▲ Lieutenant E. Anstey,
one of the 1/24th officers
killed at Isandlwana. His
body was found on the
banks of the Manzinyama
stream behind the
mountain, where he had

organized a 'last stand'.
(Ian Knight Collection)

▲ The valley of the
Manzinyama stream,
behind mount Isandlwana.
The Zulu left horn passed
down this valley in pursuit
of the survivors of the
battle: in the foreground is
one of the graves on the
'Fugitives' Trail'. Many of
the last stands took place
on the far slope, nearer the
mountain. (Ian Castle)

as the Manzimyama, chasing blindly after the fleeing N.NC. who seemed to know an escape route. The Zulus raced after them and a desperate struggle for survival developed over the rocky slopes. There are many tales of the lucky escapes, individual heroism, and horror of this tortuous journey. Many did not make it, including the gunners, whose guns became stuck in a gulley, and were overwhelmed.

Perhaps the most famous incident from the retreat concerns Lieutenant Melvill's attempt to save the Queen's Colour of the 1/24th. Melvill was the adjutant of his battalion, and it is thought that, as the line collapsed, he was ordered to take the Colour to a place of safety. He managed to fight his way across country and was joined by Lieutenant Coghill, also of the 1/24th. They descended into the steep valley of the Mzinyathi and plunged into the river which was in flood. Coghill crossed safely, but Melvill was pulled from his horse by the current, and clung to a rock mid-stream. Coghill turned back to help him, but his horse was immediately shot. Melvill was too exhausted to keep hold of the Colour and it slipped

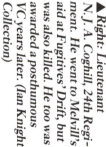

from his grasp. Together the two men managed to get across to the Natal bank and scrambled up the slope beyond. They reached a large rock and collapsed with their backs to it. There the Zulus found them and, after a sharp fight, killed them.

The camp was completely devastated. Bodies lay strewn about, black entwined with white. The bodies of the British soldiers were stripped and disembowelled in accordance with Zulu custom. Oxen and horses were killed, stores broken open and looted, tents and wagons set on fire. The Zulus took everything of value and by late afternoon they began to drift away, carrying their dead. More than a thousand had been killed and many corpses were simply dragged into dongas or nearby homesteads. Hundreds more would die later from the terrible wounds they had sustained.

▶Lieutenant and Adjutant T. Melvill, 1/24th. He attempted to save the Queen's Colour of his battalion, but was killed at Fugitives' Drift. Years later a posthumous VC was sent to his family. (Ian Knight Collection)

▶Right: Lieutenant N.J.A. Coghill, 24th Regiment. He went to Melvill's aid at Fugitives' Drift, but was also killed. He too was awarded a posthumous VC, years later. (Ian Knight Collection)

▶'Melvill's Ride to Glory': a recent study by artist Bud Bradshaw of Lieutenant and Adjutant Teignmouth Melvill, 1/24th, escaping from Isandlwana with the 1st Battalion's Queen's Colour. This picture, is more accurate than most contemporary studies, since it shows the colour furled and in its black leather case. (Reproduced by kind permission of the artist).

The casualties among the defenders were the worst ever inflicted on a British army by a native foe. Not one member of the six 24th companies survived. Of the 1,700 men who were in the camp on the morning of the 22nd, only 60 whites and 400 blacks survived.

Lord Chelmsford, meanwhile, had remained unaware of the disaster until it was over. He had arrived at Dartnell's position at about 6.00 a.m. There was no evidence of the large enemy concentration that he had hoped to find, but there was a number of small groups on the hills surrounding the Mangeni. By 9.30 these had been cleared, and Chelmsford allowed his men to take breakfast. During the meal he received the first note from Isandlwana, reporting that Zulus were advancing on the camp. He was not unduly

worried by this news, being confidant that Pulleine's force was strong enough to defend itself, and nothing unusual could be observed through a staff officer's telescope. Chelmsford sent orders for the camp to be moved forward so that the search for the main *impi* could continue. Further messages arrived during the morning, but these failed to reveal the true extent of the attack. Artillery fire was heard, and shells could be seen bursting against the Nquthu escarpment, but the tents could be seen still standing, which was taken as a sign that all was well.

Earlier in the morning, Chelmsford had ordered the 1/3rd N.N.C. under Commandant Hamilton-Browne, back to camp. They had gone a few miles when a large mass of Zulus – the left horn – swept across their front some way off. In the far distance, Hamilton-Browne could see fighting among the tents. He withdrew his men to a safer position and sent a message to Chelmsford. Chelmsford had turned with his escort to see for himself what was happening. He gave no credit to

Hamilton-Browne's stories of disaster, until a lone figure approached him and convinced him of the dreadful truth. This was Commandant Lonsdale who, suffering from heatstroke, had ridden back to the camp to secure supplies for his men who had been out all night with no food. He was dozing in his saddle, and had ridden close to the tents before he noticed the victorious Zulus ransacking them. He had managed to turn around and gallop away in the nick of time.

Chelmsford was thunderstruck. In the open, unsupported, with a hostile force between him and Natal, he had little choice but to try to retrace his steps to Isandlwana, and thence back to Rorke's

▼*Perhaps the most famous battle of the Zulu War: the defence of Rorke's Drift, 22/23 January 1879. This rather lurid contemporary print suggests something of the desperate fighting during* one of the night attacks, lit by the flames from the blazing hospital. The artist has erred in giving two Zulus (left) daggers, which were not a Zulu weapon. (Kenneth Griffith Collection)

▲ *Lord Chelmsford's force leaves Isandlwana on the morning of 23 January after a night spent on the battlefield. The appearance of the mountain is not accurate, but the the awful devastation is. (Ian Knight Collection)*

Drift. He formed his men up and began a long, slow, melancholy march back to the camp. It was dark by the time he arrived. He deployed his men in line and the artillery lobbed shells into the darkness in case the Zulus were still in possession. Three companies of the 24th were sent forward to clear the stony kopje south of the nek, then the whole force advanced. There was no opposition, for there was nothing living left in the camp. Chelmsford's men spent the night among the debris. Many found they were lying in the tall grass among the bodies of their fallen comrades. The night was interrupted by several scares, and a red glow in the sky above Rorke's Drift made matters worse. There was a fire at Rorke's Drift and the garrison was under attack.

Chelmsford had the men roused before dawn, wishing to spare them sight of the horrors that surrounded them. As they descended into the Batshe valley, an *impi* came into view on the their left. It was coming from the direction of the Oskarberg, the hill overlooking Rorke's Drift. Warily, the two sides watched each other, then passed at a safe distance, neither side seeking a confrontation. On reaching the Drift Chelmsford feared the worst, for a heavy pall of smoke could be seen hanging over the post. He sent forward some mounted men to reconnoitre and soon the sound of cheering broke out. The post was safe.

Chelmsford rode up eagerly, hoping to find that some part of the Centre Column had escaped to Rorke's Drift, but he was to be disappointed. The post had been defended with great tenacity by its original garrison, 'B' Company, 2/24th, under the command of Lieutenants Chard, RE, and Bromhead, 24th. One hundred and thirty-nine men, of whom 35 were sick, had withstood a relentless attack by 4,000 warriors for nearly twelve hours. These Zulus were members of the Undi corps, commanded by Prince Dabulamanzi kaMpande, who had been held back as the reserve at Isandlwana. They had swung wide of the right horn, taking no part in the battle, and had crossed the Mzinyathi near Fugitives' Drift. This was against the king's orders, but they were angry at having won no glory in the big battle. Chard had received an hour's warning of their approach, and had formed makeshift barricades around the mission station. The Zulu attack had begun at about 4.00 p.m. and had continued throughout the night. Having been unable to make any headway against the improvised fort, however, they withdrew at dawn on the 23rd.

Chelmsford congratulated the heroes of the fight, then left Colonel Glyn in charge to clear up the mess and secure the post, while he rode on to Pietermaritzburg, to cope as best he could with the consequences of the disaster.

W.O. LANG.

▲ *Private, Newcastle Mounted Rifles, battle of Isandlwana. Natal boasted a number of small mounted volunteer corps drawn from the settler community, each with its own uniform, which contrasted smartly with the irregulars who fought with Wood's column. They were issued with Swinburne-Henry carbines shortly before the outbreak of the Zulu War. (Wynn Owen Lang)*

▲ *A sentry of the King's Dragoon Guards on duty among the wrecked wagons on the nek. Isandlwana, June 1879. (Ian Knight Collection)*

▲ *Troops from the 2nd Division revisit Isandlwana, May 1879. Serviceable wagons are being removed while troops search for the dead amidst the debris. (Ian Knight Collection)*

THE AFTERMATH OF ISANDLWANA

The news of Isandlwana spread rapidly throughout Natal, carried by the fleeing survivors. The population, black and white, was gripped by panic, and the settlers made for the safety of improvised defensive laagers, or more secure centres such as Pietermaritzburg or Durban. For several days they feared the arrival of a Zulu army, but nothing happened. The victorious warriors had dispersed to take part in the necessary post-combat purification rituals and to recover.

From Pietermaritzburg, Chelmsford had the sorry task of sending messages to both the home government and his surviving columns, telling them of the disaster. To Wood and Pearson he could offer little advice beyond asking them to act as they saw fit, and to prepare for an attack by the entire Zulu army. With his initial invasion plan in ruins, Chelmsford must have felt despair, but he resolutely set about reorganizing his forces. It was imperative that he keep the war going while waiting for reinforcements. News of Isandlwana reached Britain on 11 February and created uproar. The government had not wanted a war, and now it had a serious defeat on its hands, but a cessation of hostilities under such circumstances was politically unacceptable, so Chelmsford would get his reinforcements.

The survivors of the Centre Column strengthened the post at Rorke's Drift, but life there was cramped, insanitary and unpleasant. Nevertheless they were able to mount a number of patrols in the direction of Isandlwana and Fugitives' Drift, and on 4 February one of these patrols found the bodies of Melvill and Coghill. Below them, among the debris trapped in the shallows of the river, they found the remains of the Queen's Colour. In March a new post was built overlooking the crossing at Rorke's Drift, and it was named Fort Melvill.

Wood received news of Isandlwana two days after the battle. Finding his camp at Fort Thinta exposed, he retired a few miles north to a new camp at Khambula. From here he continued to harass the local Zulus, and in particular the abaQulusi. It was here that Buller came into his own, constantly patrolling, skirmishing and driving off Zulu cattle. Towards the end of February, word came that news of Isandlwana had stirred republican elements within the Transvaal, and Colonel Rowlands was sent to Pretoria to guard against a possible uprising. His Column came under Wood's command, the mounted men were transferred to Khambula, and a garrison of the 80th was left at Luneburg.

On 12 March a supply convoy, escorted by a company of the 80th, which had been stranded by bad weather at Myer's Drift on the Ntombe river, was attacked by a large force of Mbilini's followers. That the preparations for defence were woefully inadequate was proved before dawn when the Zulus rushed right in among the wagons, before the escort had time to emerge from their tents and form up. There were 106 soldiers with the convoy, and 62 of them were killed, together with seventeen civilian drivers.

Buller raided the Ntombe valley as a reprisal, but failed to catch Mbilini, and Wood became convinced that stronger measures were needed.

Pearson, meanwhile, had been in Eshowe for several days when he received news of Isandlwana. He called his officers together, and after some consideration, decided to stay put. The mounted Natal Volunteers and the N.N.C. were sent back to Natal to conserve supplies, and the remaining garrison set about improving the defences. Trenches were dug, revetments built, firing steps and bastions constructed until the fort was considered impregnable. At first Pearson expected an attack daily, but it never materialized, and in fact the Zulus were content to lay siege to the post,

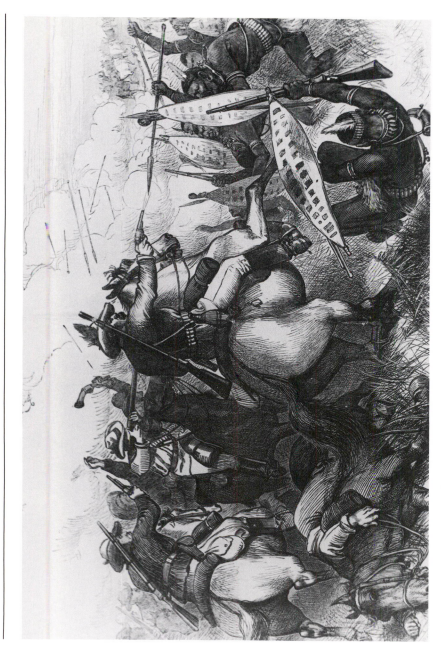

▲ A dramatic illustration of Irregulars fighting Zulus. Under Buller's leadership, Irregular cavalry constantly harried local clans in the run-up to the Khambula campaign. (Rai England Collection)

▲ The 1/24th Queen's Colour, lost at Isandlwana, was found a month later in the shallows of the Mzinyathi river. Here, the patrol returns it to the regiment at Fort Helpmekaar. (Ian Knight Collection)

hoping for the chance of a fight in the open when either Chelmsford tried to relieve it, or Pearson tried to fight his way out. Communications with Natal were cut, and skirmishes with pickets were a regular occurrence. It was only a question of time before supplies ran out, and the men's health deteriorated. A steady trickle of men succumbed to disease and were buried in a small cemetery outside the fort. Anxiously, the garrison waited for news of relief.

THE SECOND PHASE OF THE WAR

Opposing Strategies

Chelmsford's Centre and No. 2 Columns had effectively been smashed, and what remained of them was very much on the defensive. The Right Flank Column was immobilized at Eshowe, and only Wood's Left Flank Column was able to act offensively. Once the initial panic after Isandlwana had subsided, it became clear that there was to be no major Zulu incursion across the border into Natal and Chelmsford had a period of grace during which to re-organize his forces. In response to his request the home government had dispatched no less than six infantry battalions, two regiments of regular cavalry, and two more artillery batteries to South Africa. These would take several months to arrive, however, and in the meantime Chelmsford had to regain the strategic initiative.

His first task was to extricate Pearson from Eshowe, and throughout February and March he assembled a relief colum at the Lower Thukela Drift. As his preparations drew near completion he sent orders to his commanders to mount a series of diversionary attacks wherever possible along the border. Garrison commanders accordingly made a number of raids into Zulu territory, but the most serious operation was mounted by Colonel Wood. Since the attack at Ntombe, Wood had become convinced that Mbilini and the abaQulusi would have to be deprived of their mountain retreats, and Chelmsford's directive offered an ideal opportunity.

Hlobane is an irregularly shaped flat-topped plateau, whose summit is ringed by a line of cliffs broken in only a few places by rugged paths. It is the centre link in a chain of such mountains, the nearest of which, Zungwini, lay only twelve miles from Wood's camp at Khambula. Mbilini had one of his homesteads on the side of Hlobane, and it served as an abaQulusi rallying point. Wood's

The Approach to Khambula

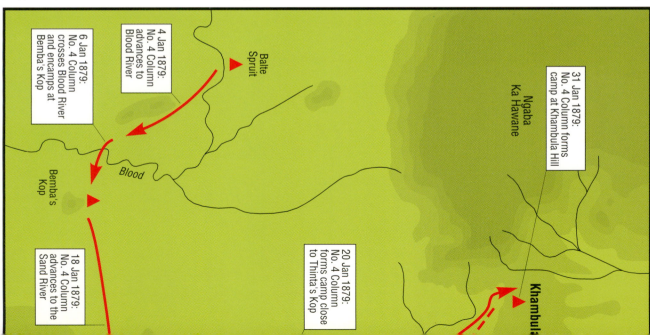

31 Jan 1879: No. 4 Column forms camp at Khambula Hill

Ngaba Ka Hawane

4 Jan 1879: No. 4 Column advances to Blood River

Balte Spruit

6 Jan 1879: No. 4 Column crosses Blood River and encamps at Bemba's Kop

Bemba's Kop

Blood

20 Jan 1879: No. 4 Column forms camp close to Thinta's Kop

18 Jan 1879: No. 4 Column advances to the Sand River

Khambula

scouts had suggested that it was possible to ascend the mountain at its western and eastern ends, and Wood planned a pincer movement to catch the abaQulusi in the middle. During the night of 27 March he sent out two parties of mounted troops, one commanded by Lieutenant-Colonel J. C. Russell, and the other by Buller, with orders to

attack the mountain at each end. Buller's men rode to the far end of the mountain and began their ascent before dawn on the 28th. They succeeded in reaching the summit despite Zulu skirmishing, and rounded up a large herd of cattle which they began to drive across the top of Hlobane towards the rendezvous with Russell.

anuary to March 1879

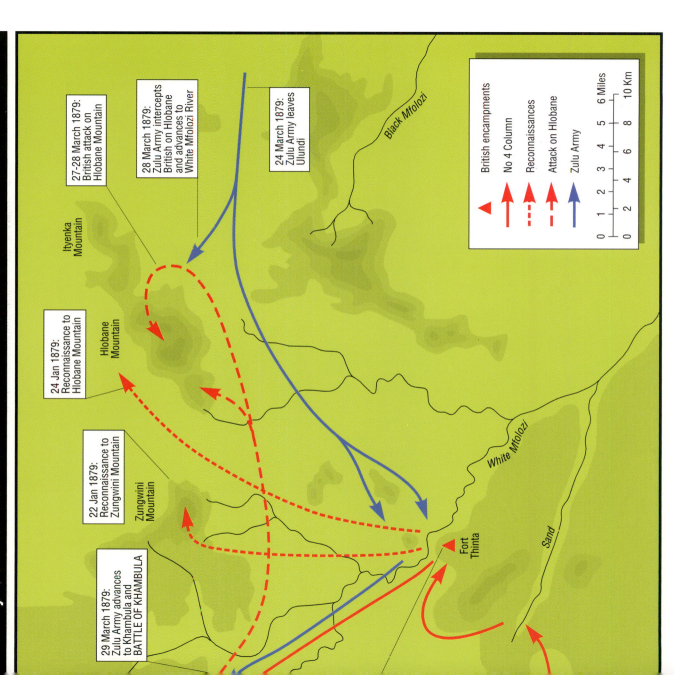

27-28 March 1879: British attack on Hlobane Mountain

28 March 1879: Zulu Army intercepts British on Hlobane and advances to White Mfolozi River

24 March 1879: Zulu Army leaves Ulundi

Black Mfolozi

British encampments
No 4 Column
Reconnaissances
Attack on Hlobane
Zulu Army

6 Miles
10 Km

Ityenka Mountain

24 Jan 1879: Reconnaissance to Hlobane Mountain

Hlobane Mountain

22 Jan 1879: Reconnaissance to Zungwini Mountain

Zungwini Mountain

White Mfolozi

Fort Thinta

Sand

29 March 1879: Zulu Army advances to Khambula and BATTLE OF KHAMBULA

▲Wood's camp on the Khambula ridge. The redoubt is in the centre of the picture, with the cattle laager below it on the right and the main laager in the foreground. Mount Zungwini is on the right skyline, and the valley occupied by the left horn is marked 'E' (right). The rocky outcrop where the iNgobamakhosi took shelter is marked 'C' (left). (Nottingham Castle Collection)

▲A group of Mounted Infantrymen from the 90th L. I., who formed Wood's personal escort, and fought at both Hlobane and Khambula. They are wearing regimental jackets, with cord riding-breeches. They are armed with the Swinburne-Henry carbine and ammunition is carried in a bandolier. (S. Bourquin)

▲A group of Irregular officers who served with Wood's Column. In the centre is Commandant Raaf of the Transvaal Rangers; the man standing left appears to be an officer of the Frontier Light Horse. That most Irregular units improvised their own uniform is is very clear from this photograph! (S. Bourquin)

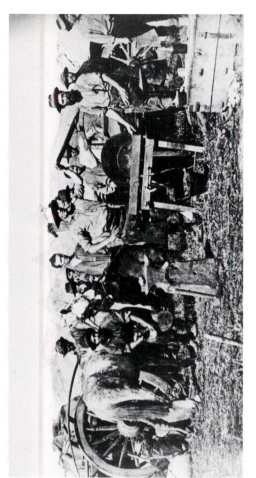

▲ The field smithy of
Buller's Horse. To the
disgust of some regular
officers, Buller's men
wore little in the way of
uniform, and were usually
distinguishable only by a
red rag wound round a
wide-brimmed hat.
(S. Bourquin)

▲ Colonel Wood (seated
centre) and his staff in the
field during the Zulu War.
Most of his officers are
wearing comfortable and
practicable blue patrol
jackets, but Wood is
wearing the scarlet
undress frock.
(S. Bourquin)

▲ Men of the
commissariat of the 90th
L.I., who were attached to
Wood's column and were
one of two infantry
battalions present at
Khambula. (S. Bourquin)

Russell, however, had been defeated by the mountain's geography, and had been unable to get his men on to the plateau. He further misinterpreted a written order by Wood, and promptly withdrew from the scene of the action altogether. Furthermore, as Buller's men rode west, they looked to their left and saw a huge Zulu army moving parallel to them in a valley some miles away to the south. This was the main Zulu army from Ulundi, and it was en route to attack Khambula. It's appearance at that time was sheer coincidence, and the worst possible luck for the British. Encouraged by the presence of the *impi*, the abaQulusi stepped up their harrying attacks and Buller was driven from Hlobane in confusion. The main army dispatched one wing to join the fight, and it cut off one of Buller's parties and all but wiped it out. Buller himself was only able to extricate his men by leading them down a steep rocky staircase subsequently christened the 'Devil's Pass'. When night fell the bodies of fifteen officers and 79 men were left on the slopes of Hlobane and the Zulus were masters of the field.

Khambula: The Opening Moves

The Zulu army which had so disastrously affected Wood's action at Hlobane had been mustered at Ulundi in the middle of March. In the immediate aftermath of Isandlwana, King Cetshwayo had tried to use his position of strength to negotiate a political settlement of the war, but he had been frustrated by his army dispersing to recuperate, and by the British determination to avenge Isandlwana at all costs. By March it was clear from increased British activity that a new phase of fighting was about to begin. The king still hoped for a diplomatic settlement, but he had to be prepared for war. In council with his generals and advisers, he decided that Wood's Column presented the greatest threat. Chelmsford's reputation as an opponent was low, and the king had been bombarded with a stream of messengers from Mbilini and the abaQulusi, begging for help against Wood. Accordingly, he decided to dispatch the main army to the north, while local forces besieging Eshowe would check Chelmsford's advance.

The king was quite specific in his instructions to the *impi*. He ordered it not to attack fortified positions, but to try to lure the troops into the open. If that failed, it was to by-pass the camp altogether, and strike into the unprotected Transvaal, in the hope that Wood would be forced out to meet it. Once again command of the army was given to Ntshingwayo, with Mnyamana accompanying it as the king's representative. A number of other important *izinduna* were present, including Zibhebhu kaMapitha, but Prince Dabulamanzi was not there. He had left Ulundi under a cloud following his unsuccessful sortie against Rorke's Drift, and, since his personal homestead was near Eshowe, he was involved in the operations against Pearson. The army itself was at least as large as the *impi* that had attacked Isandlwana and the vast majority of the warriors were veterans of the earlier battle. Far from being disheartened by the terrible casualties they had suffered at Isandlwana, they

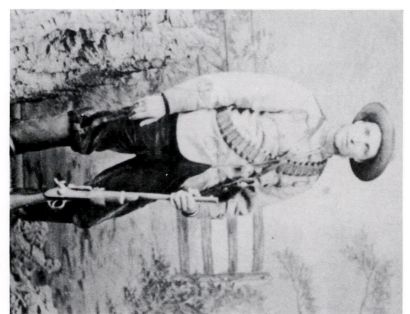

▼*An unusual photograph, thought to show the Frontier Light Horse, c. 1877. The regiment originally wore a braided buff uniform and a hat with a red puggree, but by 1879 most of its men wore civilian dress, retaining only the hat. (Ian Knight)*

W.O. LANG.

Trooper, Frontier Light Horse, Khambula. The Irregulars of the FLH proved to be tough and resiliant under the dynamic leadership of Redvers Buller, despite heavy casualties at Hlobane on 28 March. Their sortie provoked the Zulu attack at Khambula a day later, and they were particularly vengeful in the subsequent pursuit. The FLH seem to have worn either a buff braided jacket or a black patrol jacket, though many prefered civilian dress, with a red pugaree as the only uniform badge. (Wynn Owen Lang)

▲British infantry entrenching a laager in Zululand. Wood's laagers were protected by a ditch around the outside, with the soil banked up between the wagon wheels. Each wagon was chained to its neighbour and further barricaded with sacks and crates of provisions. (S. Bourquin)

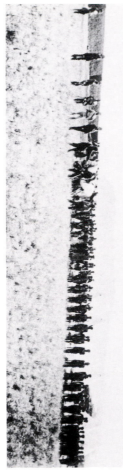

▲No. 4 Column did not include any of the battalions of the Natal Native Contingent, but did include a force of disaffected Zulus and Swazis, raised locally and known as 'Wood's Irregulars'. They were engaged at Hlobane where they were scattered, and many deserted on the night of the 28th, but about 100 remained to fight at Khambula. (Killie Campbell Library)

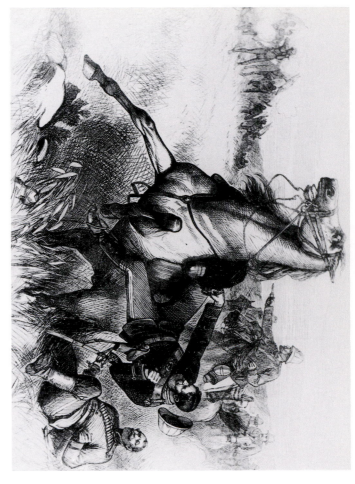

▲Zulu commanders had great difficulty in restraining their men when they were provoked to attack, so the British often used Irregular cavalry to goad them into premature and unco-ordinated attacks. (Rai England Collection)

were convinced that when they attacked in large numbers no British force could stand against them. This impression was probably enhanced by the fact that hundreds of breech-loading rifles captured at Isandlwana had been distributed amongst the *amabutho*, leading them to the belief that their fire-power was equal to that of the British. Few of the warriors shared the king's misgivings, but the fruit born of their over-confidence would be bitter indeed.

Following the action at Hlobane, the Zulus bivouacked on the White Mfolozi river, about fifteen miles from Wood's camp. If the action on 28 March had been a disaster for the British, it had at least given them ample warning of an impending attack, and Wood roused his men early on the 29th and set them to making his final preparations. His position was, in any case, a strong one, lying across the crest of a ridge the British called Khambula, but which the Zulus knew as Ngaba ka Hawana, 'Hawana's Strong-hold'. To the north the ground fell away in a bare slope towards two converging streams about a mile away; to the south it dropped into a valley in a series of rocky terraces. The eastern anchor of Wood's position was a redoubt – a ditch with the earth thrown up inside to form a parapet – which was connected by a palisade to a small laager of wagons on a flat below it, which was used as a kraal for the transport oxen. A couple of hundred yards west of the redoubt was a large defensive laager, an irregular circle of wagons chained together, with a shallow ditch and rampart thrown up around them.

To defend this position Wood had 2,086 officers and men. These included eight companies of the 90th Light Infantry, and seven of the 1/13th Light Infantry. Like Chelmsford at Isandlwana, he had no regular cavalry, but the indomitable Buller commanded 99 men of the Mounted Infantry, 165 men of the Frontier Light Horse, 135 men of the Transvaal Rangers, 99 men of Baker's Horse, 40 men of the Kaffrarian Rifles, 16 men of the Border Horse, and 74 mounted Africans (some of whom had fought at Isandlwana). These units were outside the Natal Volunteer system, and most had been raised on the Cape Frontier or the Transvaal border. They were of a decidedly piratical appear-

ance which did not always endear them to their regular counterparts, but the Frontier Light Horse in particular had earned a reputation for hard riding and tough fighting. They had suffered heavily at Hlobane, but were still a force to be reckoned with. Finally, Wood also had the services of about 180 black auxiliaries from Wood's Irre-gulars, four 7pdrs from 11/7 Battery, RA, aug-mented by two unattached guns, and eleven Royal Engineers.

All in all, it was a force comparable to Chelmsford's command during the Isandlwana campaign. Yet the outcome of the two battles was to be very different.

The Battle of Khambula

Wood's scouts spotted the Zulu army moving away from its bivouac at about 10.30 on the morning of the 29th. It appeared to be marching to the west, and for a while it seemed as it it were following the king's instructions not to attack the camp, and Wood was worried that it might be making for the unprotected Transvaal. Then it halted about four miles south of the camp and began to form up to attack. As to why the commanders were disobeying the king's orders cannot be explained with cer-tainty, but in all probability the young warriors, who made up the bulk of the force, had no time for a waiting game, and believed it their duty to attack the British as soon as possible. Once again, as at Isandlwana, a crucial battle was to be fought against the wishes of the Zulu generals.

Wood made his final preparations. He had placed two of his guns in the redoubt, supported by a company of the 90th L.I. One and a half companies of the 13th were told off to guard the cattle laager, while the remainder of the infantry and the mounted men occupied the main laager. The other four guns were placed in the open between the redoubt and the laager. As the morning wore on, and the dense Zulu masses were manoeuvring on the hills around the camp, Wood allowed his men to eat lunch. He was fully aware of the importance of the coming battle, but he appeared cool and in control, and saw no reason to make the men fight on an empty stomach. Open ammunition boxes were placed close to the lines.

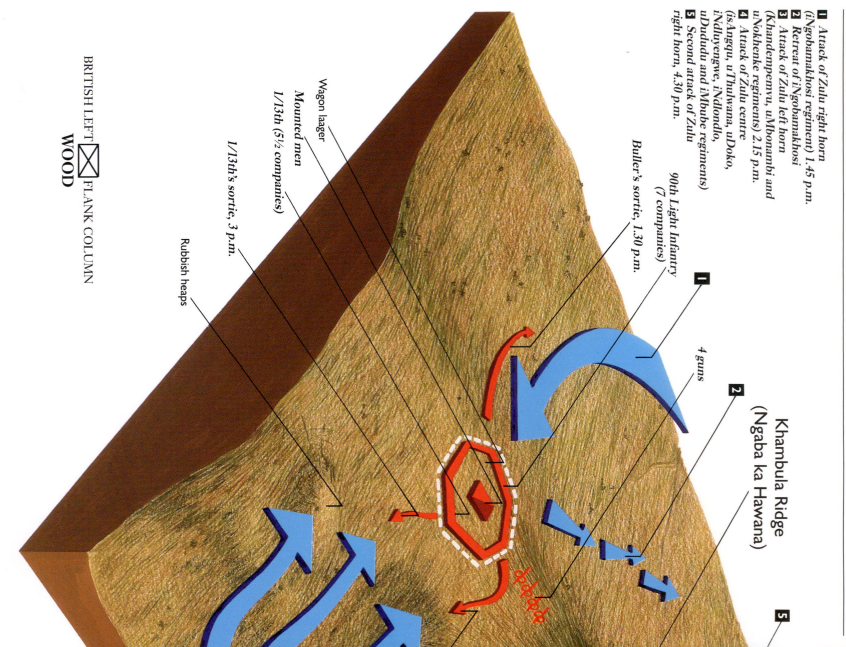

1 Attack of Zulu right horn (iNgobamakhosi regiment) 1.45 p.m.
2 Retreat of iNgobamakhosi
3 Attack of Zulu left horn (Khandempemvu, uMbonambi and uNokhenke regiments) 2.15 p.m.
4 Attack of Zulu centre (isAngqu, uThulwana, uDoko, iNdluyengwe, iNdlondlo, uDududu and iMbube regiments)
5 Second attack of Zulu right horn, 4.30 p.m.

Khambula Ridge (Ngaba ka Hawana)

90th Light Infantry (7 companies)

Buller's sortie, 1.30 p.m.

4 guns

Wagon laager

Mounted men

1/13th (5½ companies)

1/13th's sortie, 3 p.m.

Rubbish heaps

BRITISH LEFT FLANK COLUMN
WOOD

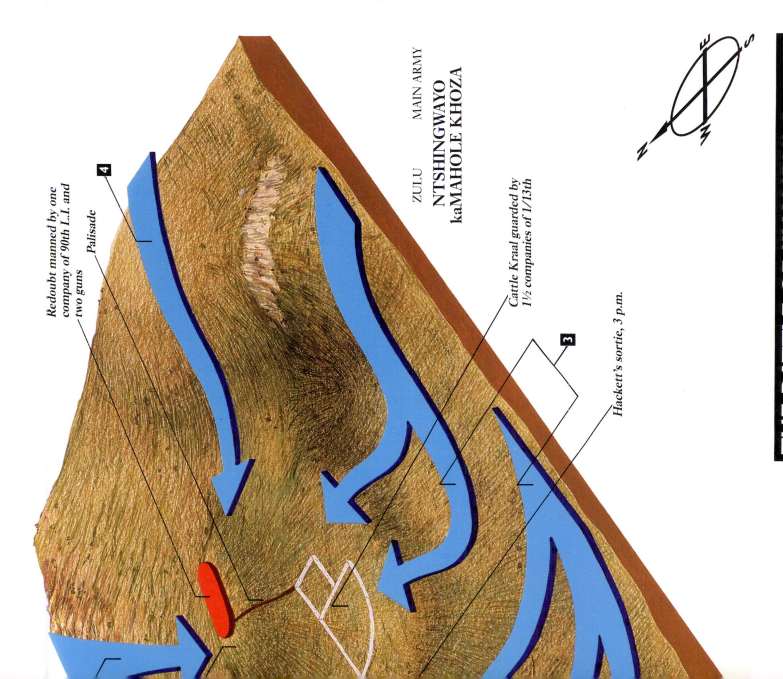

Redoubt manned by one
company of 90th L.I. and
two guns

Palisade

4

ZULU   MAIN ARMY

NTSHINGWAYO
kaMAHOLE KHOZA

Cattle Kraal guarded by
1½ companies of 1/13th

3

Hackett's sortie, 3 p.m.

THE BATTLE OF KHAMBULA

**The Zulu attacks and the British sorties, 1.30 to about 5.30
p.m., 29 March 1879**

Then, at about 12.45 p.m., he ordered the tents struck in preparation for the fight.

By that time, the Zulus were almost in position. The left horn (Khandempemvu regiment) moved towards the valley to the south of the camp, while the chest (the uMbonambi, iNdlondlo, uDududu, is;Angqu, uThulwana, iMbube and iNdluyengwe regiments) ascended the eastern spurs of the ridge. The iNgobamakhosi regiment, which comprised the right horn, swung round to the north of the camp. The regular *amabutho* had been augmented by a large number of Qulusi clansmen from the local district, and the huge masses stretched for more than ten miles from tip to tip. To more than

one anxious observer inside the laager, it seemed that the hills were black with warriors.

Curiously, considering it had had farthest to march, the right horn came into action first. It had halted its advance about a mile and a half from the camp, while the chest and centre were still moving into position. Wood was increasingly concerned that a coordinated attack by such a large force would be more than his firepower could withstand, but he needn't have worried. At about 1.30 the iNgobamakhosi suddenly moved forward, and drew up in battle formation – a dense mass screened by clouds of skirmishers – less than a mile away. Apparently the warriors believed that the rest of the army was also advancing to attack; or perhaps they were vying with other regiments for the honour of being first into the red-coat camp. Certainly, it was not a move ordered by Ntshingwayo, who had taken up a position about 700 yards east of the redoubt, and who was apparently scarcely able to control his forces. In

any case, Wood seized his opportunity, and ordered Buller to make a sortie to provoke the iNgobamakhosi into an unsupported attack.

The ground over which the first dramatic phase of the battle would take place sloped away from the laager towards a patch of marshy ground which marked the sources of the streams. It was completely bare grass, with no cover except for dozens of ant-heaps which scattered the slope like low boulders. Buller's sortie consisted of roughly a hundred men, and they rode to within comfort-

▼ *Buller's sortie against the Zulu right horn at Khambula; the opening* *shots of the decisive battle of the War. (Ian Knight Collection)*

▶ Two 7pdrs from an unidentified battery, photographed with Wood's Column later in the War. Wood had four guns of Major Tremlett's battery, and two unattached ones, at his disposal. Because the Zulu attacks were not coordinated, he was able to move them to meet each fresh threat. (S. Bourquin)

▲ Sergeant, 1/13th Light Infantry, Khambula. Unlike the majority of infantry battalions, the Light Infantry wore their rank chevrons on both sleeves, rather than on the right sleeve only. Chevrons were white for NCOs below the rank of sergeant. Sergeants also carried a sword bayonet for the Martini-Henry rather than the usual triangular-section socket bayonet. The 90th's uniform would have been the same, apart from the difference in facing colour (buff for the 90th); the 90th did not, however, wear the facing colour on the cuff of the undress frock coat, which was therefore plain red. (Wynn Owen Lang)

▶ Lieutenant F. Nicholson, RA, who commanded the two guns stationed in the redoubt at Khambula. He was directing the fire from an exposed position at the parapet when he was wounded. He died the next day. (Ian Knight Collection)

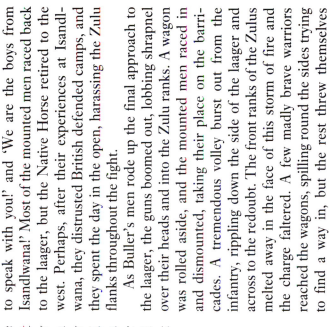

able rifle-range of the stationary warriors. Here they dismounted and loosed a volley. The effect was electric; with a great shout of the war cry 'Usuthu!', the Zulus surged forward. Buller's men hastily mounted up and fell back, pausing every fifty yards or so to deliver another volley. Several times the furious Zulu charge swept to within a few paces of the stragglers, but each time Buller managed to extricate his men. The Zulus called out in frustration 'Don't run away Johnny, we want

to speak with you!' and 'We are the boys from Isandlwana!' Most of the mounted men raced back to the laager, but the Native Horse retired to the west. Perhaps, after their experiences at Isandlwana, they distrusted British defended camps, and they spent the day in the open, harassing the Zulu flanks throughout the fight.

As Buller's men rode up the final approach to the laager, the guns boomed out, lobbing shrapnel over their heads and into the Zulu ranks. A wagon was rolled aside, and the mounted men raced in and dismounted, taking their place on the barricades. A tremendous volley burst out from the infantry, rippling down the side of the laager and across to the redoubt. The front ranks of the Zulus melted away in the face of this storm of fire and the charge faltered. A few madly brave warriors reached the wagons, spilling round the sides trying to find a way in, but the rest threw themselves down behind what pathetic cover they could find. They were terribly exposed, however, and could not sustain this position, and they reluctantly fell back, taking cover behind a rocky fold in the ground to the north-east.

They left the slope behind them strewn with bodies.

By provoking the attack of the right horn and defeating it, Wood had gained a tremendous tactical advantage. He had disrupted the Zulu plan, and it would be difficult now for them to avoid squandering their strength in uncoordinated piecemeal attacks, while he, in turn, would be free to concentrate his fire wherever it was most

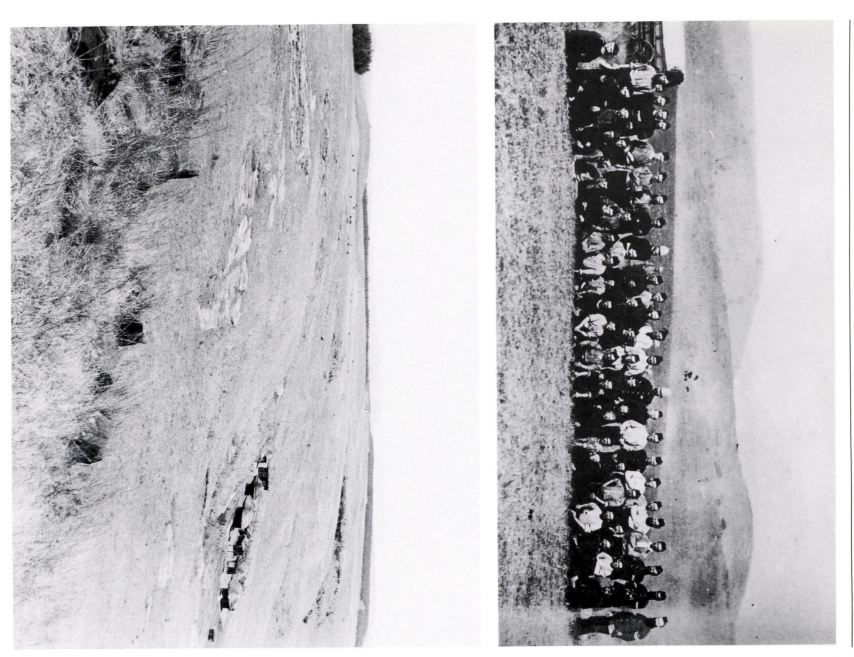

▲A company of the 1/13th, photographed on the Ulundi campaign. The cattle laager was manned by men of the 13th, who were driven out for a while by warriors of the uNokhenke ibutho. (S. Bourquin)

▲Below: the southern approaches of the Khambula camp. The

laager was near the trees, and the rise on the horizon marks the site of the redoubt. The ground drops away steeply to the right, and the Zulu left horn was able to mass in safety, charging up the slope centre. Hackett's men formed up at the top of this slope. Ian Knight Collection)

There was a flurry of hand-to-hand fighting with the men of the 1/13th stationed there, and the Zulus forced their way in. The kraal was still full of cattle, and the mêlée continued among the herd, which was surging and bellowing in fright. The British troops were in a dangerous position and Wood sent a messenger to order them to fall back. He and his staff took up a conspicuous position below the redoubt to encourage and support the men during the retreat. The jubilant uNokhenke poured into the positions they had vacated, and opened a heavy, but inaccurate, fire on the laager.

Exploiting this success, Zulu commanders could be seen frantically urging a new wedge of warriors into position on the slope. These were men of the uMbonambi *ibutho* and their attack threatened to punch a hole into the heart of Wood's defences. The rocky terraces prevented his fire from striking into the valley, so Wood ordered Major Robert Hackett of the 90th to take out two companies of his regiment and break up the Zulu concentration. To leave the protection of the laagers was a very risky business, but Hackett's men advanced swiftly and in good order, taking the Zulus by surprise. They formed up in a line at the top of the slope, and began firing steady volleys down into the valley. These chopped great swathes through the tightly packed uMbonambi, who gradually fell back before them, scrambling back into the valley or for the cover of the rocky outcrops on either side.

Hackett's sortie probably saved the day for Wood, but his men were completely exposed to Zulu return fire. Wood ordered the artillery and infantry in the redoubt to rake the cattle-laager, and the uNokhenke were gradually driven out, but a few snipers were still able to enfilade his line from the left. Worse, he came under a heavy cross-fire from his right, the extreme tip of the Zulu left horn. This, the Khandempemvu (umCijo) regiment, had pushed forward as far as the lip of the ridge to the west of the camp. A company of the 1/13th dashed out and drove them back with the bayonet, preventing them from forming up, but the British could not maintain this position, and the Zulus took possession of a small knoll about three hundred yards from the laager. This was the site of a camp rubbish dump, and was covered by a

needed. The whole movement had lasted less than three-quarters of an hour, and as the iNgobamakhosi fell back, so the left horn and chest moved rapidly forward in a belated attempt to support them. The chest came on in great waves, rippling over the contours, the warriors holding their shields high of the grass as they surged towards the redoubt. Their approach was hardly less open than that of the iNgobamakhosi, however, and the artillery opened up with shrapnel which blasted great gaps in their lines. At 800 yards the infantry opened fire, and by the time the distance closed to 300 yards, the devastation wrought in the ranks had been appalling. Nevertheless the centre pressed up almost to the walls of the redoubt before falling back.

It was the Zulu left horn which proved the most dangerous, however. Here the warriors could advance along the southern face of the camp, completely sheltered from fire by a steep, grassy valley. At the western end a small stream had cut a slope which offered a route up to the crest of the ridge. It opened out between the two laagers, almost in the centre of the camp. The Zulus could mass in the valley then charge up the slope, out of reach of British fire until they crested the rise less than a hundred yards from the laager. When they did so, of course, they ran into a hail of fire that was devastating at so close a range. The heavy Martini-Henry bullets sent warriors somersaulting back into their ranks, or tumbling over one another, but they kept coming, buoyed up by a very real hope of success. At about 3.00 p.m. a series of determined charges made Wood aware of the danger. The uNokhenke *ibutho*, on the left of the Zulu centre, moved down into the valley and carried on right up to the walls of the cattle kraal.

W.O. LANG.

▼Left: Major R. Hackett. His sortie was a turning-point in the Battle of Khambula, but he was severely wounded in the head by Zulu sniper fire. (Royal Collection)

▼Lieutenant A. Bright, 90th L.I. He was wounded during Hackett's sortie, a bullet striking his thigh and passing through to his other leg. In the confusion of the battle, the surgeons failed to notice the extent of his injuries and he bled to death. (Ian Knight Collection)

▼Hackett's sortie: his men line the crest of the slope and fire down at the warriors massing in the valley. The redoubt is on the rise, centre; the main laager is to the left. The number of casualties in this sketch suggest how vulnerable Hackett was to Zulu enfilading fire. (Ian Knight Collection)

▲Major Robert Hackett, 90th Light Infantry. Hackett led the sortie of two companies of his regiment that broke up the Zulu left horn. He received a serious head wound during the retreat. We have shown him in the officers' undress frock coat, with regimental facing colour on the collar, and the collar badge and cuff braid of a major. (Wynn Owen Lang)

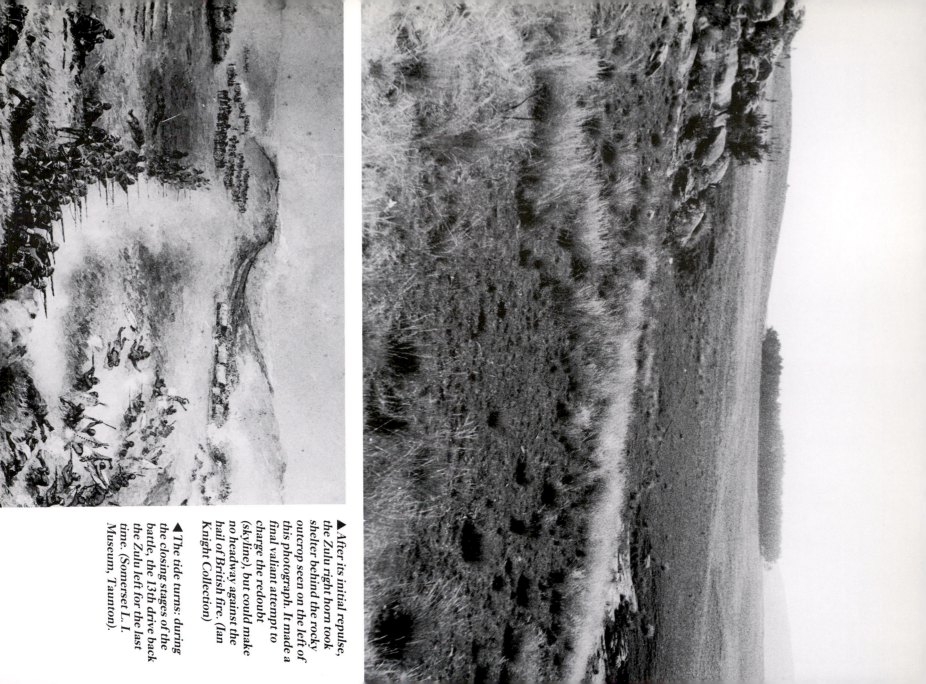

▲After its initial repulse, the Zulu right horn took shelter behind the rocky outcrop seen on the left of this photograph. It made a final valiant attempt to charge the redoubt (skyline), but could make no headway against the hail of British fire. (Ian Knight Collection)

▲The tide turns: during the closing stages of the battle, the 13th drive back the Zulu left for the last time. (Somerset L.I. Museum, Taunton).

heap of manure which had sprouted a covering of tall green grass. Warriors from the regiment dived into the grass and opened a galling fire at close range on both Hackett's men and the southern face of the laager. As the bullets began to strike down amongst the 90th men, several were hit. Hackett's subaltern, Lieutenant Bright, fell shot through both legs, and a minute later Hackett himself was hit in the face. Wood recalled the sortie and the men carried back their wounded officers. Hackett was to survive, though he lost the sight of both eyes; the surgeons failed to notice the extent of Bright's injury, and he bled to death during the night.

In the main laager, Redvers Buller noted the danger posed by the riflemen in the rubbish dumps and organized counter-fire. He urged his men not to waste time aiming at individual warriors, but to fire into the soft dung. The bullets passed clean through and struck the warriors behind. Volley after volley obliterated the heaps, and the Zulu fire was suppressed. The next day sixty-two bodies were found amongst the debris.

The narrow failure of the Zulu assaults on the south of the camp, and the success of the British sorties, was probably the turning-point of the battle, but there were to be several hours' hard fighting to come. The Zulu chest regrouped and advanced again and again along the crest of the ridge, each succeeding assault jockeying for a better position. On one occasion they came almost within reach of the artillery horses, in the open between the laagers, and in another the dead fell against the very wall of the redoubt. Each attack met with the same result, however; a concentrated storm of fire which nothing could withstand

At about 4.30, the iNgobamakhosi, on the Zulu right, having recovered from the shock of its initial repulse, came forward again. It was a spirited charge that surged out from the cover of the rocky outcrop and dashed towards the northern face of the redoubt. But the final approach to the ramparts was steep, and as the warriors struggled forward a furious rain of musketry and shrapnel fell on them, scything them down. The charge collapsed.

It was as if the Zulu tide had reached high-water mark. The warriors crouched or lay in a great semi-circle, taking whatever cover they could, surrounding the camp on three sides, firing their inadequate firearms. Now and then an *induna* would urge one regiment or another to screw up their courage for a final rush, but none was able to close. By 5 o'clock it was clear to Wood that the day was his, and he ordered a sortie of the 13th to clear the cattle laager of any surviving warriors. A company of the 90th was pushed out to the lip of the valley again, forming up where Hackett's men had once stood. They drove a few lingering

HEROISM AT THE BATTLE OF KAMBULA

▶ *The original caption of this montage of incidents from the battle is 'Heroism at Khambula', and it is honest enough to include Zulu bravery. A warrior stabs himself (left) rather than die at the hands of a British sortie. In the centre a wounded man is snatched to safety in front of the Zulus during Buller's sortie, while (right) a wounded man is succoured during the retreat from the cattle laager. (Ian Knight Collection)*

warriors out at bayonet point, and then began to fire down into the dark masses beginning to drift away down the valley. Everywhere, the Zulus were beginning to retire. For the most part they went slowly and in good order, still firing and carrying their wounded. The British infantry shouted and cheered as they went.

Now was the moment for Wood to close in for the kill. He ordered Buller to chase the warriors from the field, and his men hastily mounted and streamed out of the laager in pursuit. The Irregulars had suffered heavily in the Hlobane débâcle of the day before, and they were in no mood to be merciful now. The effect of their charge on the disheartened Zulus was shattering. Any cohesion that remained collapsed under the pressure and the retreat dissolved into a rout. A few Zulus turned and fought, but most were utterly exhausted. Many were so tired that they could not run, and some simply turned and stood, inviting their tormentors to shoot them down. Some even stabbed themselves rather than die at the hands of the British. The Irregulars were only too happy to be granted the opportunity for such slaughter. They shot warriors down at close range, 'butchering the brutes all over the place', as one officer later commented. Some even snatched up Zulu spears to skewer the warriors more efficiently. A few warriors tried to hide in long grass or ant-bear holes, but all were spotted and killed. 'The slaughter continued for as long as we could discover any human form before our eyes,' wrote another participant. Later, when details of the butchery reached the British press, they caused something of an outcry, yet in truth Wood had been given a golden opportunity to deliver a stunning blow to the Zulu army and he would have been foolish to pass it up. Nor could his troops have been much restrained in any case; they knew only too well that there was no quarter given in Zulu warfare, and they were hell-bent on revenge. Someone saw Buller himself in the thick of the fight, 'like a tiger drunk with blood'.

The chase continued to the slopes of the Zungwini mountain, about twelve miles away. In the early stages, the Zulu commanders made some attempt to rally their men. Mnyamana Buthelezi urged them to turn around once the British had emerged from their laager, but Zibhebhu pointed out that it was hopeless. Once the rout had begun, there was no stopping it. Mnyamana tried to lead part of the army away, back to Ulundi, but most of the warriors would not follow him, and simply fled towards their homes. It is not known for certain

▶ *The Zulu snipers in the rubbish heaps at Khambula. For once the Zulus were able to make the most of their firepower and effectively enfilade British sorties. Figures 1 and 2 are of the Khandempemvu (Mcijo) regiment, and are wearing the minimal war-dress of the later battles. Before the war, most Zulu guns were either Brown Bess flintlock patterns 2 or percussion models, but the Martini-Henrys captured at Isandlwana markedly improved the range and accuracy of Zulu fire. Figure 3 is one of Mbilíne's followers, wearing an 80th Regiment jacket taken at Ntombe. Figure 4 represents a senior Zulu commander. His status is suggested by his single crane feather and lourie plume, and by the necklace of red beads and leopards' claws, worn only by important men. He also wears a 'bravery bead' necklace and a full waist-kilt. He has a revolver taken at Isandlwana: a number of officers' personal weapons were recovered after Khambula. The Zulu seem to have carried them more as trophies than for use. (Angus McBride)*

▶ *As the Irregular cavalry emerge from the laager to chase the Zulus from the field, a warrior fires a last defiant shot. The Zulu retreat began in good order, but the Irregulars turned it into a rout. (S. Bourquin)*

how many casualties they had suffered, but when the British burial parties began to collect the dead, 785 bodies were brought in from the immediate confines of the camp. Many were badly knocked about by shell fire. They were buried in large pits 200 feet long, 20 feet wide and 10 feet deep.

Because of the severe nature of the pursuit, the ratio of killed to wounded was probably very high. Hundreds more lay out along the route of the retreat, and bodies kept turning up for days, hidden behind rocks or in tall grass where they had crawled to die. Of those who managed to escape, bearing the terrible wounds inflicted by the heavy

lead bullets, few probably survived the journey to their family homesteads. Many men of rank and influence had been killed, for the officers had exposed themselves a good deal in leading the charges. Most of the dead were from the younger regiments, and the nation was to be stunned by their loss. Perhaps as many as 3,000 warriors died in total, and it is impossible to calculate the number who survived with minor injuries.

By comparison, Wood's losses were insignificant: eighteen NCOs and men killed, and eight officers, 57 NCOs and men wounded. Ten of the wounded later died and they were all buried in a

▲ A British cavalry patrol searches out a Zulu fugitive. The ruthless British pursuit after Khambula inflicted heavy losses and scattered the Zulu army. (Rai England Collection)

▶ Commandant F. Schermbrucker of the Kaffrarian Rifles, one of the Irregular units which took part in the pursuit. Of it he wrote, 'We took the assegais from dead men, and rushed among the living ones, stabbing them right and left with fearful revenge for our misfortunes.' (Killie Campbell Library)

Zulus were capable of mounting a successful attack on the camp, until it was too late. His tactical decisions were based not only on this false premise, but also on poor Intelligence work. Thus he allowed his command to be split, and the further division between Durnford and Pulleine compounded this error. When the fighting began, the Zulus had the initiative and caught the British scattered over a wide area. Pulleine did not have the chance to do anything but react to their attacks. His opening dispositions were based on a mis-understanding of the threat – like everyone else, he believed the main army to be miles away confronting Chelmsford – and the Zulus never gave him the chance to correct his mistake. They won because they had out-generalled their enemy and caught them on the wrong foot.

Wood, who is held by many to have been a better general than Chelmsford, was nevertheless just as capable of under-estimating his enemy, as the Hlobane shambles proved. After Isandlwana, however, it was very clear to everyone in the British force that a massed Zulu attack had to be taken seriously. Wood had a day's warning of the attack on Khambula and he made the most of it. His camp was securely entrenched, and he was able to plan his dispositions knowing exactly the sort of attack he would face. Whereas Pulleine's firepower was scattered and diluted, Wood's was concen-trated to devastating effect. Zulu commanders were extremely adept at spotting enemy weak-nesses, but Wood left nothing to chance. Kham-bula was a rock on which the Zulu army dashed itself to pieces.

The extraordinary courage of the Zulus in attacking both camps should not be under-estimated. They sustained horrifying casualties at Isandlwana, but if they were disheartened, they were prepared to face British fire yet again in the belief that they could triumph in the end. Their own firepower was increased in the second battle, yet it made no difference to the outcome, and in the final analysis success still depended on coming to close quarters with the enemy. This was exactly what Wood prevented them from doing. The defeat was a particularly bitter one, because after Khambula the Zulu survivors understood that they were no match for the enemy.

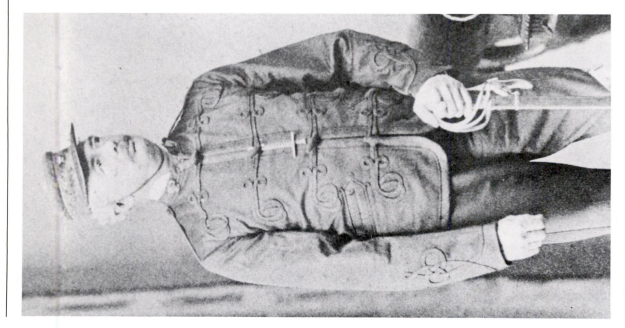

small cemetery to the north of the camp.

There are a number of instructive comparisons to be drawn from the battles of Isandlwana and Khambula. There was not, on the whole, a great deal of difference in the troops involved in either campaign. Lord Chelmsford and Colonel Wood had commanded columns of roughly equal strength and, for the most part, the same Zulu warriors fought in both battles. Why then were the results so different?

There is no doubt that Chelmsford's over-confidence was a contributing factor to the disaster at Isandlwana. He simply could not accept that the

AFTERMATH

It was immediately apparent to both sides that the Zulu defeat at Khambula was of the greatest strategic importance. The victors of Isandlwana had been faced head on, and been crushed. British confidence was restored while Zulu morale collapsed. The *impi* would never again take the field with quite the same determination, and many warriors simply stayed at home for the duration of the war. King Cetshwayo, when he heard the news from his dispirited commanders, realized straight away that a successful military solution to the war was simply no longer an option. His view was confirmed a few days later with the report of a fresh defeat in southern Zululand.

On the same day that Wood had been engaged at Khambula, Lord Chelmsford had crossed the Thukela with the Eshowe relief column. On 2 April he had been attacked by an *impi* consisting largely of local troops near the site of the burnt-out military kraal of Gingindlovu. Chelmsford's men had formed a square and thrown up a ditch and rampart about it, and the Zulus had once again been unable to penetrate the wall of fire. The next day Eshowe was relieved. Chelmsford decided not to hold the post, and he began to evacuate the garrison, which had withstood three months of siege. By the end of the month most of his men were back in Natal and he was more or less back where he started in January.

His reinforcements had been arriving, steadily, however, and Chelmsford planned a new campaign. He stuck to his original idea of advancing in several columns, but each column was much stronger, and they were to act in close co-operation with one another. The main thrust was to come from the new Second Division, which advanced from the border hamlet of Dundee and joined the old route of the Centre Column some miles beyond the fateful field of Isandlwana. Wood's column was to remain largely intact, but it was now to be called the Flying Column, and it was to move down to link up with the Second Division. The remaining column, the First Division, was to pacify the coastal strip.

The troops were in their start positions by the end of May, and the so-called Second Invasion began. The business of supplying the troops remained as much a nightmare as it had during the first invasion, and the advance was marked by a series of forts built as depots, and to protect the lines of communication. Cumbersome wagon trains constantly shuffled between them, tying down hundreds of troops on escort duty. The Zulus may have been reluctant to mount a full-scale attack in the open, but they harassed patrols and advance parties by sniping and ambush.

The new invasion had scarcely begun when it suffered a new disaster. The exiled Prince Imperial of France, Louis Napoleon, heir to the Bonapartist throne, who was attached to Lord Chelmsford's force as an observer, was killed while on patrol. The final advance took place in the face of constant skirmishing.

There was also an increase in diplomatic activity. King Cetshwayo sent repeated messages to Chelmsford, asking his terms. Chelmsford, knowing that Sir Garnet Wolseley was en route to replace him, demanded unconditional compliance with the terms of the Ultimatum. Cetshwayo was no more able to comply with that in June 1879 than he had been in January; nor did Chelmsford expect otherwise. He was hoping to win one final battle in an endeavour to restore his tarnished reputation.

It took place on 4 July. Chelmsford led the men of the Second Division and the Flying Column across the White Mfolozi river, and drew them up in a large square opposite the king's residence at Ulundi. Here the Zulus made their last dramatic gesture of defiance. More than 20,000 warriors

The Second Invasion of Zululand, May to July 1879

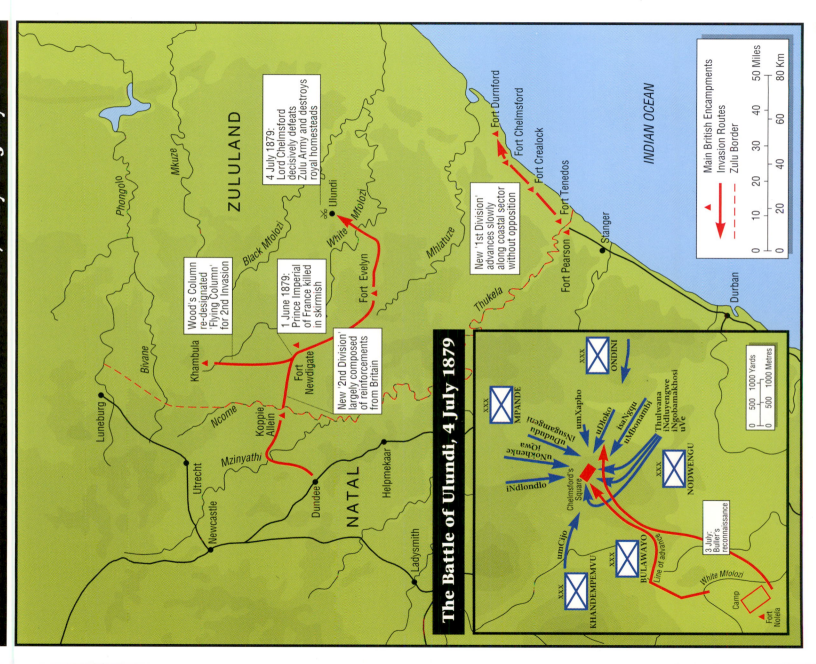

ZULULAND

Mkuze

Phongolo

Bivane

Luneburg

Utrecht

Newcastle

Ncome

Mzinyathi

Koppie Allein

Dundee

Helpmekaar

Ladysmith

NATAL

Black Mfolozi

Khambula

Fort Newdigate

White Mfolozi

Fort Evelyn

Ulundi

4 July 1879: Lord Chelmsford decisively defeats Zulu Army and destroys royal homesteads

Wood's Column re-designated 'Flying Column' for 2nd Invasion

1 June 1879: Prince Imperial of France killed in skirmish

New '2nd Division' largely composed of reinforcements from Britain

Mhlatuze

Thukela

Fort Durnford

Fort Chelmsford

Fort Crealock

Fort Tenedos

Fort Pearson

Stanger

Durban

INDIAN OCEAN

New '1st Division' advances slowly along coastal sector without opposition

Main British Encampments
Invasion Routes
Zulu Border

0   10   20   30   40   50 Miles
0   20   40   60   80 Km

The Battle of Ulundi, 4 July 1879

ONDINI

MPANDE

XXX

umXapho

uDloko

isaNgqu

uMbonambi

Thulwana
iNdluyengwe
iNgobamakhosi
uVe

nNokhenke
iQwa
uDududu
iNsugangeni

iNdlondlo

Chelmsford's Square

NODWENGU

XXX

umCjo

KHANDEMPEMVU

XXX

BULAWAYO

XXX

Line of advance

White Mfolozi

3 July: Buller's reconnaissance

Camp

Fort Nolela

0   500   1000 Yards
0   500   1000 Metres

from right across the kingdom had mustered for the last great battle. They attacked with great daring, but their cause was lost before it began. After half an hour their charges petered out, and the 17th Lancers chased them from the field.

The British withdrew from Zululand as soon as the war was over. King Cetshwayo was hunted down, captured and sent into exile in Cape Town. Chelmsford returned home and was greeted as a conquering hero, though he never commanded troops in action again. Wood and Buller went on to pursue their successful careers, and spent a good deal of time fighting Africans the length and breadth of the continent. Buller was finally humbled by the Boers during his bungled attempts to relieve Ladysmith in 1900.

And Zululand? Once victory had been won, a new home government had no compunction in abandoning Frere's policy of Confederation. No attempt was made to annex the country taken at the cost of so much blood. Instead it was broken up into thirteen petty kingdoms and distributed amongst Africans thought to be loyal to Britain. Within a few years it had dissolved into civil war. Cetshwayo was brought out of exile and given part of his own kingdom in an attempt to restore order, but he was defeated by Zibhebhu kaMapitha, who had become his implacable rival. He died in 1884. During the next twenty years there were two rebellions aimed at overthrowing white influence, but both were ruthlessly suppressed. Today Zululand is part of the Republic of South Africa.

▼ The final defeat of the Zulu army: the battle of Ulundi, 4 July 1879. In the final analysis, Zulu courage and fighting spirit were every bit as good as those of the British, but, as this picture suggests, British firepower was crushingly superior. (Rai England Collection)

▼ The effect of Martini-Henry volley fire: a group of warriors cut down in a clump. This sketch was made at Ulundi, but there were many such scenes at Khambula, where the Zulus suffered terribly from British firepower. (Ian Knight Collection)

▶ King Cetshwayo was captured at the end of the War and sent into exile at Cape Town where he was lodged – as this photograph shows – at the castle. The post-war settlement of Zululand was such a disaster, however, that part of his old territory was restored to him. He was defeated in the civil war that followed and died in 1884. (Keith Reeves Collection)

THE BATTLEFIELDS TODAY

For any one interested in the Anglo-Zulu War, a trip to the battlefields offers a fascinating chance to see them largely unchanged by the passing of more than a century. In some sectors commercial farming has altered the landscape, but the two battles featured in this book, Isandlwana and Khambula, look almost as they did when brave men crossed rifle with assegai, seeking to destroy or defend a royal dynasty. There are a number of organized tours, based both in the UK and South Africa. A good set of maps, such as the Laband and Thompson *Field Guide*, is essential for anyone exploring on his own, as Zululand is still quite rugged in places!

The nearest modern town to Isandlwana is Dundee — which for the military historian is interesting in itself, being the site of the Boer War battle of Talana — and from here it is 5 kilometres to the junction with the R68 Nquthu road. Follow this towards Nquthu, a distance of about 45 kilometres, then turn right, following the R68 towards Babanango. About 14 kilometres along this road is a turn off to the right leading to Isandlwana, a further 10 kilometres away.

Your first view of the battlefield is as this dirt road crests the lip of the Nquthu plateau and begins to descend to the plain. This is the view the attacking *impi* would have had, and it is worth stopping here and walking to a high-point, a knoll named Itusi, on the left. From here one can see the whole area of the Isandlwana campaign, from the distant Oskarberg on the right, round to the new camp site at Mangeni on the left. The road dips past the spot where the rocket battery came to grief, skirts the Conical Kopje, and crosses the donga where Durnford made his stand. It then runs up to the nek beneath Isandlwana, where much of the fighting took place. Leave your car here and explore the camp site, where there are a number of monuments to the fallen, and numerous

white-washed cairns that cover their bones. A road leads across the front of the mountain towards the small settlement of St. Vincent's. Here a foot-track leads up to the spur, where Mostyn and Cavaye were posted. Back on the plain, one can walk out to the firing line, which is a surprisingly long way from the camp. It is easy to imagine how exposed the men must have felt. Walking back to the mountain and ascending the lower slopes, one finds a large cairn marking the spot where Captain Younghusband made his last stand. This position gives a good view of the battlefield as a whole. Behind the mountain, a line of cairns marks the trail to Fugitives' Drift.

Moves are currently under way to ensure the preservation of the battlefield and to prevent any encroachment on the site by expanding local settlements. It is intended to move the current road, making it less obtrusive, and establish a visitors' centre at St. Vincent's. A new school for local children is to be built. These additions will not damage the dignity of the area, but will aid visitors in their understanding of the battle. Only by standing on the slopes of Isandlwana and experiencing the brooding atmosphere is it possible to appreciate the factors which shaped the decisions of that fateful day in January 1879.

The most suitable base for exploring the battlefield of Khambula is the town of Vryheid in northern Natal. Driving out of Vryheid, follow the R33 Paulpietersberg road and after 12 kilometres turn left along a dirt road, the D486, to the site of the battle. Passing through a farm gate, the road runs along the southern base of the redoubt and curves right to the military cemetery. The best overall view of the battlefield can be gained from the redoubt itself. From here you can see in all directions. The area has hardly changed, apart from a wattle grove which grows near the site of the main laager, where the British guns once stood. Having taken in the general view, one can examine specific areas of the battlefield. Walking away from the redoubt, crossing the track, you will see a valley open up before you, lined in places with cliffs. This is where the Zulu left horn advanced, completely sheltered from British fire. Turn to the right and you will see the slope where the valley runs up to the ridge. This is where Hackett made his sortie. There is a Zulu homestead nearby, and above it is the knoll where the Zulu snipers took shelter. Following the track one passes the laager side, and winds down towards the cemetery where British soldiers killed in the battle are buried. From here one can walk across the north face of the laager and redoubt. The country is just as open as it was during the battle, and it is easy to imagine the terrifying ordeal of the right horn, as it ran up the slopes in the face of withering fire. This ascent is deceptive; viewed from the redoubt, it appears gentle, but viewed from the Zulu position, the final stretch is a stiff climb, and the redoubt towers above you on the skyline. There are still antheaps on the site, and their inadequacy as cover is a poignant reminder of the plight of those brave warriors.

Of the other sites connected with the war, Hlobane and Ntombe are largely unchanged, but Nyezane and Gingindlovu, nearer the coast, are in the heart of the sugar-cane district and have been affected accordingly. There is little at Gingindlovu to remind one of the battle other than a small cemetery. The battlefield of Ulundi is largely surrounded by the rapidly growing capital of KwaZulu. The site of Chelmsford's square is marked by an ornamental garden which contains the graves of British troops killed in the battle, and

by a large dome. Plaques on its walls constitute what was, for many years, the only memorial to the Zulu dead. Nearby is the site of King Cetshwayo's Ondini homestead (an alternative name for Ulundi, and so called to distinguish it from the modern town), where archaeologists have reconstructed some of the huts over the original floors. The complex also holds the Museum of Zulu Cultural History. Perhaps the most famous site of the war, Rorke's Drift, is still a working mission and there are a number of modern buildings on the site. Plans are progressing, however, to develop a museum on the site of the original defensive position, the exact location of which has been recently determined by archaeologists.

As well as the battlefields, there are numerous forts marking the British advance, and a scattering of lonely graves, each with a story to tell. **Note:** If you are interested in visiting the battlefields, you may like to know that the authors of this book organize regular tours, which visit all the sites connected with the war. For further details, write to Ian Castle, 49 Belsize Park, London, NW3 4EE.

Battlefield Relics

The issue of removing relics from South African battlefields is currently the subject of intense debate, following the illegal excavation of part of Khambula, and the subsequent sale of relics. Readers are advised that it is ILLEGAL to dig on South African battlefields, and hefty fines may be imposed on anyone found guilty of breaking this law.

CHRONOLOGY

11 December 1878: Ultimatum delivered to Zulu representatives.

6 January 1879: No. 4 Column crosses River Ncome into Zululand.

11 January: Expiry of Ultimatum.

11 January: No. 3 Column crosses into Zululand at Rorke's Drift.

12 January: No. 1 Column begins to cross into Zululand at Lower Thukela.

12 January: No. 3 Column attacks Sihayo's stronghold.

17 January: Main Zulu army leaves Ulundi to attack No. 3 Column.

20 January: No. 3 Column arrives at Isandlwana.

22 January: Battle of Nyezane; No. 1 Column defeats 6,000 Zulus.

22 January: Battle of Isandlwana.

22/23 January: Battle of Rorke's Drift.

24 January: No. 4 Column receives first news of Isandlwana.

27 January: No.1 Column receives news of Isandlwana.

28 January: No. I Column decides to hold Eshowe.

31 January: No. 4 Column moves camp to Khambula Hill.

11 February: Chelmsford's dispatch detailing defeat at Isandlwana reaches London.

11 February: Communications with Eshowe cut.

3 March: Heliograph communication opened between Thukela and Eshowe.

11 March: First reinforcements authorized by UK government arrive.

12 March: Attack on 80th Regimental convoy at Ntombe river.

28 March: Battle of Hlobane; mounted troops of No. 4 Column defeated.

29 March: Advance of Eshowe Relief Column.

29 March: Battle of Khambula.

1 April: Prince Imperial of France arrives in Natal to join Lord Chelmsford's staff.

2 April: Battle of Gingindlovu. Eshowe Relief Column defeats large Zulu army.

3 April: Eshowe relieved.

11 April: Last of Chelmsford's reinforcements arrive.

13 April: Chelmsford reorganizes his forces into 1st Division, 2nd Division and Flying Column.

21 May: Reconnaissance in force to Isandlwana, bodies buried except those of 24th. Wagons removed.

31 May: 2nd Division crosses into Zululand.

1 June: Prince Imperial killed in ambush while on patrol.

16 June: Chelmsford receives news that he is to be superseded by Sir Garnet Wolseley.

17 June: Flying Column and 2nd Division link for advance on Ulundi.

20 June: 1st Division advances from depots previously established in southern Zululand.

20 June: Bodies of 24th Regiment at Isandlwana buried.

27 June: Combined 2nd Division and Flying Column arrive at Mthonjaneni heights, for final march on Ulundi.

28 June: Sir Garnet Wolseley arrives in Durban.

1 July: 2nd Division and Flying Column camp on White Mfolozi river.

4 July: Battle of Ulundi; final defeat of the Zulu army.

8 July: Chelmsford resigns his command.

15 July: Chelmsford hands over command to Wolseley.

28 August: Capture of King Cetshwayo.

A GUIDE TO FURTHER READING

The Zulu War is perhaps the most written about of all British Colonial wars, so there is plenty of reading material from which to choose. Donald R. Morris's classic *The Washing of the Spears* (New York and London 1965) is still essential reading, although more research has questioned Morris's interpretation of Isandlwana, and has shed more light on Zulu political and military structures. Ian Knight's *Brave Men's Blood* (London, 1990) presents a comprehensive and balanced history of the war, giving equal weight to the Zulu perspective, and is lavishly illustrated. It also includes a detailed review of the literature of the war. The leading academic historians of the war are John Laband and Paul Thompson, and much of their work has been collected in *Kingdom and Colony at War* (Pietermaritzburg, 1991). Their *Field Guide to the War in Zululand and Defence of Natal* (revised edition, Pietermaritzburg 1987) includes the best selection of maps available, and is also an essential guide to visiting the sites. Eye-witness accounts can be found in Frank Emery's *The Red Soldier* (London, 1977). A useful general history of Zululand, from Shaka through to the 1906 Rebellion, is T. V. Bulpin's *Shaka's Country*(Cape Town, 1952). The organization and uniforms of the rival armies are considered in two Osprey Elite titles, *British Forces in Zululand 1879* and *The Zulus*, both by Ian Knight, and illustrated by Rick Scollins and Angus McBride respectively. Howard Whitehouse's *Battle in Africa* (London, 1989) presents a useful picture of the way Colonial campaigns were organized on the continent.

INDEX

(References to illustrations are shown in **bold**.)